BEAUFIGHTERS OVER BURMA

BEAUFIGHTERS OVER BURMA

No. 27 Squadron, RAF, 1942-45

DAVID J. INNES

BLANDFORD PRESS
POOLE · DORSET

First published in the UK 1985 by Blandford Press,
Link House, West Street, Poole, Dorset BH15 1LL

Copyright © 1985 David J. Innes

Distributed in the United States by
Sterling Publishing Co. Ltd,
2 Park Avenue, New York, NY 10016

British Library Cataloguing in Publication Data

Innes, David J.
   Beaufighters over Burma. No. 27 squadron, RAF,
   1943-'5.
   1. Great Britain. *Royal Air Force. Squadron, No. 27*
   2. World War, 1939-1945—Aerial operations,
   British   3. World War, 1939-1945—Campaigns
   —Burma
   I. Title
   940.54'4941   D786

ISBN 0-7137-1599-5

Typeset by Poole Typesetting (Wessex) Ltd.
Printed in Great Britain by R. J. Acford

CONTENTS

FOREWORD

To be asked to write a Foreword to this account of the life and times of a remarkable Royal Air Force squadron operating under all conditions (good and bad – mostly bad!) on the Burma Front during the 1943-44 period of World War Two, is a great privilege which I value more than I can say. I only wish I could do full justice to such an inspiring story – more particularly as I feel a 'fatherly' interest in No. 27 Squadron, having re-formed it in 1942 with Beaufighter aircraft and commanded it in its formative and developing months.

World War Two has now fallen back into the past and most people under the age of 50 or so will know little about it, and even less about what it was like to be in a front-line squadron in the hot and steamy jungles of Eastern Bengal – the oppressive heat, the appalling weather conditions during the monsoon period, the lack of anything to do when not actually flying, the flies, the mosquitos, the other creepy crawlies – but nonetheless, and in spite of this, the wonderful esprit de corps which existed, not only among the aircrew, both officers and NCOs but also among the other unsung heroes, the groundcrews who kept the aircraft serviceable under the most rigorous and difficult conditions one could possibly imagine. Nevertheless, there was much happiness among all the members of the squadron under even these trying conditions.

Much has been written about the Burma Campaign against the Japanese. In this book the author has captured the spirit of one of the Royal Air Force units which fought this war. He has not, however, made it a 'dry' matter of history with facts and figures and statistics. He has successfully achieved a balance between the necessary information on flying operations and the human aspect of life in an operational squadron. No doubt, much the same story could be told about any squadron on this front, but the author has put the work of the squadron in the context of the war situation at the time and the strategy of Higher Authority, thereby showing how and why the squadron's operations and the targets for those operations fitted into the overall waging of the war on this front. The squadron had a uniqueness about it, however, as it was, during 1943, virtually the only squadron operating consistently over Burma throughout the monsoon period, thus providing the Allies with the ability to harass the enemy continuously.

The author was a pilot with No. 27 Squadron – in fact, he flew his first operational sortie as my number two – and this has enabled him to write the story of the squadron's part in the Burma Campaign in an authentic manner – not an easy task considering that he resides in Australia and has had to do much of the research by correspondence with the United Kingdom. I know this did present him with some problems and his effort in overcoming them is to be highly commended.

August 1983   Group Captain H. C. Daish, OBE, RAF, (Rtd)

SOURCES AND ACKNOWLEDGMENTS

Unlike many air force squadrons, No. 27 Squadron does not have an active association by whom squadron histories could be held, and I said to myself in 1981 that if someone does not record the role of the squadron in the Burma Campaign of World War Two, then an interesting part of the squadron's history may be lost. I have never previously attempted to write a book and it took some motivation, so I only hope it will not be 'too disappointing to the ear', as I believe a story of this nature should be as factual as possible.

Of necessity, I found the story developing into two themes, one about the squadron and the other about the Burma Campaign generally. In respect of the Campaign, I am indebted to the following publications: *Wingate's Phantom Army,* by W. G. Burchett (1944); *Wings Of The Phoenix,* produced by the British Air Ministry (1949); and *The Forgotten Men,* Iain Adamson (1965). In respect of the squadron, my special thanks to the members of the squadron who provided valuable background material, as well as to members of Nos. 31, 60 and 194 Squadrons.

People in the British Ministry of Defence, the Imperial War Museum, the RAF Museum and the Public Records Office, London, have been most co-operative and their help did encourage me to visit the United Kingdom to further the research.

The book *The Sky Belongs To Them* by Wing Commander Winfield, DFC, AFC, (William Kimber & Co. Ltd.), and the contribution of British Aerospace plc, Bristol, are thankfully acknowledged.

Finally, special thanks to my wife, Bobbie, for putting up with the disruptions I have caused to a normally placid household. Fortunately, she has a love of flying going back to pre-war when she did considerable flying as a passenger in a de Havilland Hornet Moth.

INTRODUCTION

The campaign in Burma, especially in the years 1942-44, was often referred to as 'the forgotten war', and India and China were rated very low on the Allied scale of priorities, despite the fact that names such as Alexander, Wavell, Auchinleck, Mountbatten, Giffard, Slim, Peirse, Baldwin, Williams, Stilwell, Old, Merril, Chennault and Chiang-Kai-shek were synonymous with the Allied efforts to recapture Burma. However, Allied servicemen who took part in the campaign at the time had no knowledge of the politics that were being played between the British, Americans and Chinese. The conflict between the American support for the half-hearted role China was playing against the Japanese and the British desire to see amphibious landings on Rangoon, the Malay Peninsular and the Dutch East Indies was a festering sore that had to be healed before Burma could be re-occupied.

Whilst these Allied triangular wranglings were taking place from late 1942 to 1944, Burma became a very fragmented theatre of war. The British forces faced the Japanese in the Arakan and the north-western border of Burma with India. The Americans, operating from the very north of Burma, were convinced that the highest priority should be given to the construction of a road linking Ledo in north-eastern India with the Burma Road running east from Mandalay into China. Pending this road link, the assistance to China – and, in particular, for Chennault's 'Flying Tigers' in China – was by C-47 Dakotas and C-46 Commandos which carried vital supplies from air-strips in the Brahmaputra Valley in north-eastern India 500 miles over 'The Hump', a 15,000-foot mountain range, into China. It was against this backdrop that an Allied decision was made in September 1942 to establish No. 27 Beaufighter Squadron, RAF, to operate in the Burma Campaign. The story about the squadron mainly covers the period late 1942 to March 1944.

The author was an Australian pilot with the squadron during this period and carried out thirty-six sorties. He was more fortunate than several of his squadron mates who made the supreme sacrifice.

Recent books such as *Bomber* by Len Deighton and *Bomber Command* by Max

11

Hastings have highlighted the early years of the war in Europe and the part that the RAF bombers of 1940 played – the Blenheims, Hampdens, Wellingtons, Whitleys. The days of the 'heavies' and the philosophy of bombing European cities was still to come.

The story about No. 27 Squadron's involvement in the Burma Campaign has a certain similarity to the RAF bomber squadrons of 1940 in Europe. Both were guinea pigs in respect to the expertise that was later developed through experience. Experience in the Burma theatre meant acclimatising to tropical conditions – heat, change of diet, etc. – for the aircrews and ground crews from the United Kingdom, determining aircraft tropical tolerances and understanding monsoon weather, if that was possible.

In *Wings Of The Phoenix* – the official story of the air war in Burma – the Air Ministry broadly mentions the part Beaufighters played in 1943 and in particular during the monsoon period from May to October. Likewise, *The Flying Elephants* by Chaz Bowyer outlines the history of No. 27 Squadron, which was originally formed during World War One, and includes a section dealing with the role of the squadron in the Burma Campaign.

In 1976, Dr Roland Winfield, DFC, AFC, an RAF medical officer who, rather uniquely for one of that profession, also obtained his pilot's wings and flew the equivalent of three operational tours with many RAF squadrons, released a book titled *The Sky Belongs To Them*. One complete chapter of the book, 'Nicolson and the Beaufighters', is a direct reference to No. 27 Squadron in the Burma campaign and will be referred to in this story.

As the chapters unfold, the author will recount the part played by No. 27 Squadron in the sometimes referred to 'forgotten war' of 1942-45. No doubt this tag was understandable to those controlling war-time priorities in London and New York, but to those in the field in India and Burma it was an impression we had to learn to live with and get on with the job.

Personal research with No. 27 Squadron members who are still alive has proved a difficult task some forty years later. With the author living in Australia and many of the squadron members coming from the British Isles, two from Canada, one from New Zealand, and six from Australia, this can be understood.

However, thanks to references to No. 27 Squadron in publications about the 1939-45 war, access to some log books of squadron aircrews, photographs, co-operation from those members of the squadron whom I have been able to contact, and official records, it has been possible to record what I hope the reader will find to be an interesting account of the war-time activities of an RAF long-range attack fighter squadron in a theatre of war that did not attract the publicity of the European or Pacific theatres. Inevitably, there is a degree of autobiography which seems difficult to avoid in books of this nature. However, the author's prime purpose was to write a book which would provide interest for those who were there, and one from which relatives and friends might learn something of the conditions of the Burma Campaign in general, and of the role played by No. 27 Beaufighter Squadron in particular.

It was a fact of Royal Air Force life in the 1939-45 war that the Empire Air Training Scheme brought together thousands of young men from many countries with a common purpose. We shared good fellowship, happiness and sadness in each other's company for a short period of time, and as suddenly as we came together so did we part, to find ourselves back in our own countries where life was rather different from when we had left it a few years earlier.

It was perhaps paradoxical that when we joined up in the early days of the 1939-45 war, whether in the UK, Australia, Canada, New Zealand or South Africa, we all expected to finish up in the UK or Middle East fighting the Germans and Italians. However, Japan's entry into the war in December 1941 – which led to the entry of the USA – changed all that and what we did see were squadrons of mixed nationality aircrews simultaneously operating in Europe, the Middle East and the Far East against two very different types of enemy.

The story will take the reader through the activities of the squadron during an interesting period of the Burma Campaign. For the reader to appreciate these activities the first chapter provides a background to the Japanese occupation of Burma and the second chapter a background history of No. 27 Squadron and what was involved in putting Empire Aircrew Trainees into a powerful wartime machine – the Bristol Beaufighter. Through my personal involvement, I hope I have been able to bring to light how the squadron ticked, and, in so doing, get away from a completely statistical account of its operational achievements. In other words, to tell how a group of young wartime airmen from different countries thrown together in strange surroundings learnt to co-ordinate their individual talents and develop a team spirit that, in some small way, contributed to the Allied victory against the Japanese in 1945.

1·BURMA BACKGROUND

The invasion of Burma by the Japanese commenced with bombing attacks on Rangoon on 23 and 25 December 1941: exactly twelve months later Beaufighters of No. 27 Squadron made their first attack against the Japanese. The first Japanese raid on Rangoon was by fifty to sixty bombers escorted by thirty fighters against which the Allies put up sixteen Brewster Buffaloes and fourteen Curtiss P-40 Tomahawks. RAF records show that nine bombers and one fighter were shot down for the loss of two Tomahawks in the air, and four Tomahawks and five Buffaloes on the ground. The second raid by about 100 bombers and fighters was opposed by thirty Buffaloes and Tomahawks. RAF records show that at least seventeen Japanese aircraft were shot down for the loss of four Allied fighters. It was estimated that there were 7,000 civilian casualties from the two raids because the Burmese did not take shelter.

In December 1941, the British were hard pressed by the Germans and Italians in the European and Middle East theatres of war, and, although they had only just become an active ally, the Americans too were hard pressed by the Japanese in another theatre of war – the Pacific.

Burma in the eyes of both the British and the American Commands was, perhaps understandably, a low priority, but to the Japanese it was the very opposite. By occupying the port of Rangoon then occupying Burma itself, the Japanese saw the means of cutting off supplies for China and for a long cherished dream of invading India. In so doing they would benefit from Burma's main resources, oil and rice, as well as gaining protection for recently occupied Siam (now Thailand).

There was no road from India into Burma and no army, they believed, could reconquer Burma from the north – but they had overlooked the air.

Supplies for China before the Japanese invasion were by ship to Rangoon then by rail along the Irrawaddy Plains to Mandalay. From there, the Burma Road made its way north-east through the mountains of the Northern Shan States before crossing into China. Work on extending the railway beyond Mandalay had been completed as far as Lashio, some 150 miles, and further work taking in the boundary between Burma and

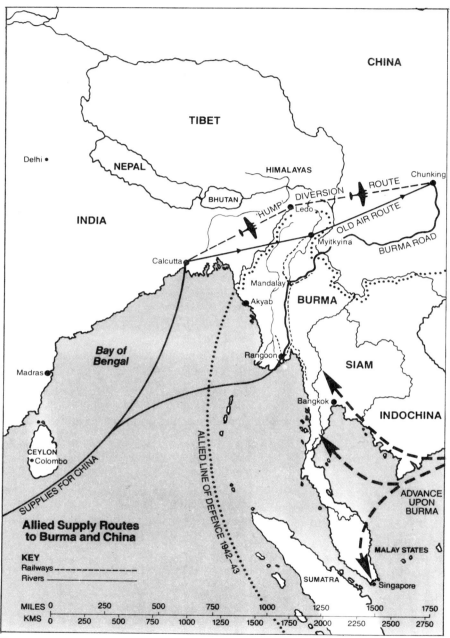

The Allied supply lines to China and Burma at the time of the Japanese invasion of Burma in December 1941, and the famous 'Hump' route.

China was in progress when Allied hostilities with the Japanese broke out. In all, it was an overland journey of 1600 miles from Rangoon to Chungking, and more than half the distance entailed crossing high mountains which in places exceeded 10,000 feet.

The secondary supply line to China was by ship to Calcutta thence by air to Chungking, with a refuelling stop at Myitkyina in northern Burma.

This then was the picture at the end of 1941. Whilst the Burmese were bewildered by the Japanese onslaught on their country and the Allies were puzzled by the determination of the Japanese to capture Burma, it soon became obvious that their motives and ambitions were very purposeful. Tragically, the Allied forces were so pitiful that it was just a matter of time before the Japanese achieved their objective of capturing Burma and establishing large numbers of troops along the Burma/India borders in the Arakan and Northern Burma.

The Allied ground forces in Burma, although numbering some 25,000 combat troops, were mostly partly trained recruits. The air strength was No. 67 Squadron, RAF, with sixteen obsolescing Brewster Buffalo fighters, with a further sixteen reserve aircraft commanded by Squadron Leader R. Milward. It was supported by the twenty-one Curtiss P-40 Tomahawks of the 3rd Squadron, American Volunteer Group (AVG) – The 'Flying Tigers' – commanded by Arius Olson. At the time, there were fifty-five Tomahawks in Burma at Toungoo about to leave for China, but Chiang-Kai-shek agreed to the re-deployment of twenty-one to Rangoon when it was recognised that the defence of that port was of more vital importance than was combatting the Japanese in China. Obviously, if Rangoon could be held, then China's main supply base would continue to operate. In addition, a flight of Indian Air Force Westland Wapiti and Hawker Audax was available for reconnaissance and a Burma Air Force flight of DH Moths for communication and four Bristol Blenheim Mk Is of No. 60 Squadron, RAF.

There was an early Allied command plan to provide Burma with six fighter squadrons, seven bomber squadrons, two Army co-operation squadrons and a general reconnaissance squadron – a total of 280 aircraft. However, on 12 December 1941, Air Vice Marshal D. F. Stevenson, CBE, DSO, MC, the AOC No. 2 Group Bomber Command, RAF, United Kingdom, was told he was to take over as AOC Air Force Burma. This command would consist of four fighter squadrons, six bomber squadrons and one general reconnaissance squadron. As it turned out, three fighter squadrons equipped with Hawker Hurricane Mk Is, Nos 17, 135 and 136, did reach Burma during the campaign, but their strength never exceeded that of two squadrons. One Bristol Blenheim Mk IV bomber squadron, No. 113, arrived from Egypt on 7 January and, notwithstanding the long flight, nine took off at 2 am next day to bomb the dock area of the capital of Siam, Bangkok. One of the pilots, Flying Officer G. W. N. Bassingthwaighte, an Australian, subsequently joined No. 27 (Beaufighter) Squadron as a flight commander (Squadron Leader, DFC) in January 1944. A second Blenheim

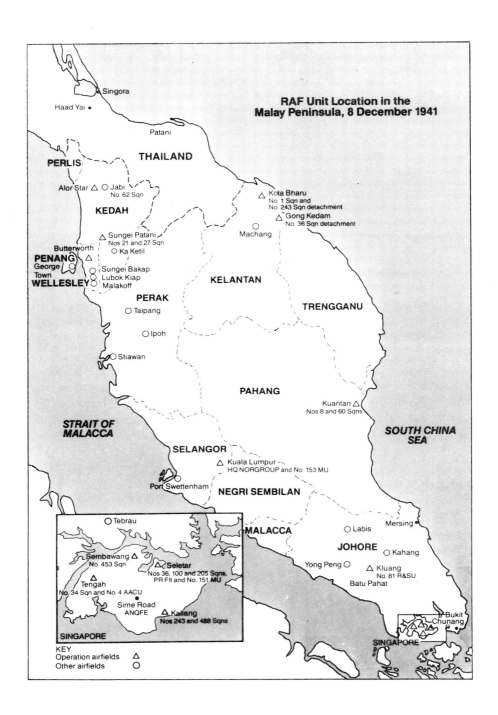

RAF Unit Location in the
Malay Peninsula, 8 December 1941

Singora

Haad Yai

Patani

PERLIS

THAILAND

Alor Star △ ○ Jabi
No. 62 Sqn

KEDAH

Kota Bharu
No. 1 Sqn and
No. 243 Sqn detachment
△ Gong Kedam
No. 36 Sqn detachment

Machang

△ Sungei Patani
Nos 21 and 27 Sqn
○ Ka Ketil

Butterworth
PENANG △
George
Town
WELLESLEY

○ Sungei Bakap
○ Lubok Kiap
○ Malakoff

PERAK

○ Taipang

KELANTAN

TRENGGANU

○ Ipoh

○ Stiawan

PAHANG

Kuantan △
Nos 8 and 60 Sqns

STRAIT OF
MALACCA

SELANGOR

△ Kuala Lumpur
HQ NORGROUP and No. 153 MU

SOUTH CHINA
SEA

Port Swettenham

NEGRI SEMBILAN

○ Tebrau

MALACCA

○ Labis   Mersing

JOHORE   ○ Kahang

Sembawang △
No. 453 Sqn

△ Seletar
Nos 36, 100 and 205 Sqns,
PR Flt and No. 151 MU

Yong Peng ○   △ Kluang
                No. 81 R&SU
Batu Pahat

△
Tengah
No. 34 Sqn and No. 4 AACU

Sime Road
ANQFE

△ Kallang
Nos 243 and 488 Sqns

SINGAPORE

Bukit
Chunang

SINGAPORE

KEY
Operation airfields   △
Other airfields   ○

18

Mk IV bomber squadron, No. 45, arrived in February but at no stage did the effective strength of the Blenheims exceed that of one squadron.

The Japanese invaded Burma by coming in from the north-west of Siam, first crossing the Siam/Burma border on 13 December and, by the 15 December, had occupied Victoria Point. They had the advantage of supply lines to their armies that moved along the rivers and roads that followed the troughs between the mountains and across the plains that make up the lower part of Burma. After the two bombings of Rangoon at Christmas, the Japanese strategy was to capture Moulmein in lower Burma which would give them access to the Salween River. This they did on 31 January. Simultaneously, they renewed their bombing attacks on Rangoon and, over a period of six days, more than 200 aircraft were employed in an attempt to wipe out the Allied air forces. More than fifty Japanese aircraft were destroyed and Rangoon was held, at least temporarily.

Moving further north, the Japanese quickly reached the Sittang River where heavy ground fighting, with diminishing Allied air participation, occurred. Once the Sittang was lost, Rangoon was doomed, but it was essential it be held long enough to allow landing of the 7th Armoured Brigade and 150 tanks. This was achieved against heavy odds in the air. At the end, an almost extinct Allied fighter force was facing some 250 Japanese aircraft. The demolition of docks, oil installations and equipment began on 7 March, and Rangoon was evacuated next day. Rangoon's airfield at Mingaladon had already been evacuated and all flyable aircraft moved north to hastily constructed dirt strips at Zigon, then to 'Park Lane' and finally to the established Magwe airfield some 200 miles from Rangoon. Here a new wing – BURWING – was created, commanded by Group Captain M. S. Broughall, MC, DFC, and comprising the remnants of Nos 45, 60 and 113 (Blenheim) Squadrons, the remnants of Nos 17, 67 and 136 (Hurricane) Squadrons, and the remainder of the 3rd Squadron, AVG. Lord Louis Mountbatten visited Magwe and addressed all air force personnel on the polo club grounds. He told them that it was necessary to retire further to a good defensive position in order to continue the fight.

Simultaneously, AKWING, under Group Captain N. C. Singer, DSO, DFC, was formed at Akyab on the Arakan coast, comprising No. 135 (Hurricane) Squadron, No. 139 (Blenheim Mk V) Squadron, a Hudson reconnaissance flight and a small communications flight. The remaining Blenheims of No. 113 Squadron had been flown back to Calcutta and, when replacement aircraft arrived from the Middle East and Britain, it was intended that the squadron would become a part of the AKWING force.

Following a successful attack by BURWING on their old base at Mingaladon on the morning of 21 March, when sixteen Japanese aircraft on the ground and eleven in the air were destroyed by nine Blenheims of No. 45 Squadron escorted by ten Hurricanes from Magwe, the Japanese retaliated and over the next twenty-four hours some 230 aircraft dropped more than 200 tons of bombs on Magwe. All that remained of BURWING was six Blenheims, eleven Hurricanes and three Tomahawks, and these were immediately withdrawn – the Blenheims and Hurricanes to Akyab and the Tomahawks to Loiwing in the north of Burma.

Over the next few days, Japanese aircraft repeatedly attacked Akyab and practically obliterated what remained of the Allied air force. Thus, by the end of March 1942, the RAF had been driven from its last operational base in Burma.

Back in the Irrawaddy delta the Japanese ground forces were moving northwards rapidly. Mandalay fell on 3 April, the Chinese army to the east had broken and less than half of the original Allied 25,000 combat troops were all that remained. India was a long way off – and the monsoon season was approaching! There could be no ground relief for these forces: they simply had to fight a delaying retreat.

Air evacuation from Burma was mainly from the northern village of Myitkyina, the refuelling point on the old airline route from Calcutta to Chungking. Myitkyina finally fell to the Japanese on 7 May, and of the 8,616 wounded, ailing and weak men, women and children that were evacuated, most were flown out from Myitkyina. This evacuation was mainly by C-47 Dakotas and C-46 Commandos of the RAF, Chinese Air Force and the US Army Air Force. Of this number of evacuees, no less than 4,000 were flown out by No. 31 Squadron, RAF.

In the retreat from Burma it is not known how many Burmese started in the south, but about 400,000 reached India at the end of a 1,000 mile march. Other uncounted hosts of refugees headed for the high mountains to the north-east and eventually China. On 20 May, what remained of the British and Indian troops reached Imphal in the State of Manipur, India, just before the monsoon broke, effectively closing the roads and tracks over which they had just marched.

The Allies had anticipated that, sooner or later, Japan would enter the war. In preparation for this eventuality, a special British commando unit was formed, which became the 204 Military (Commando) Mission to China. Its story is one that should be mentioned. It was planned to play an important role should Japan enter the war but it turned out to be a tragic exercise. The unit was established during 1941 at Maymyo, a hill station to the east of Mandalay. There the station's Bush Warfare School prepared it for guerilla warfare.

Originally there were five cadre battalions, each of 150 men. When Japan declared war, they were to move into China to become the sabotage experts of the five battalions of Chinese guerilla troops which, Chiang Kai-shek said, were operating behind the Japanese lines. By blowing up bridges, mining roads and destroying outposts the guerillas would force the Japanese to keep thousands of trained soldiers in China in order to guard their lines of communication. The damage the guerillas could do would be out of all proportion to their numbers.

Such a task needed men of character, intelligence and physique. Some such men

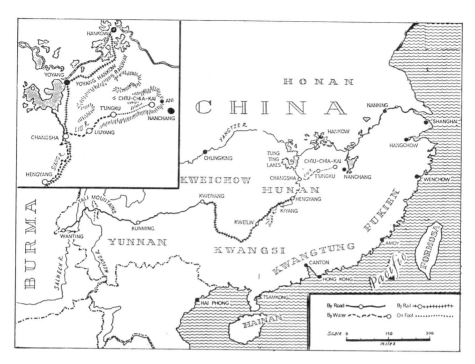

The route of 204 Military (Commando) Mission (from *The Forgotten Men*).

arrived, mostly from disbanded commando units or as volunteers, but many commanding officers used the guerilla school as a dumping ground for their undesirables, warrant officers and NCO's, and private soldiers. Some were returned to their regiments; the guerilla school did as best as it could with the others, for there was a shortage of men.

When Japan declared war, two cadre battalions were rushed to the Burma-Siam border, while the three remaining battalions, Burma, Malaya and Australia – named after the army commands from which most of the men had come – were stripped to fifty men apiece. On 21 January 1942, the Burma battalion set out for China in eleven trucks. On 23 and 25 January, the other two battalions followed.

After literally forcing their way past the Chinese guards at Wanting on the Burma-China border they travelled thousands of miles by lorry, train, junk and sampan in a period of nine months. First, they travelled the Burma Road in their own lorries through the Tali Mountains, past Kunming and on to Kweiyang where the railway to the east began. They travelled by train through Kweilin and Kiyang on to Hengyang.

Then a most arduous journey was made by junk and sampan along the fast flowing Siang and Lui Rivers, past Changsha and Tungku to Ch'iu-Chia-Kai, resulting in the loss of many commandos who now were suffering from shortages of food, clothing, ammunition and medical aid.

In the official history of the war against Japan it says that 204 Mission was withdrawn from China 'since they were not being properly used by the Chinese'. In actual fact, after nine months in China with little more than a recognition by the Chinese that they were present, they were operationally unable to carry out the task originally assigned to them.

After they reached Ch'iu-Chia-Kai two events occurred which really decided the future for the commandos. The Australian ambassador, Sir Frederick Eggleston, after his visit to the Mission while they were still at Kiyang, had cabled his Government imploring them to withdraw the Australians no matter what the British Government did. News that there were Australians in China had burst in Australian newspapers, because in his diplomatic bag Sir Frederick had sent out some letters from the troops to their relatives.

One of the Mission officers, Major Ian Robinson, had been evacuated to Chungking en route to India to have an operation. Here he met the British attaché, Brigadier Grimsdale, who arranged for him, en route to hospital, to stop off in New Delhi to meet Sir Archibald Wavell, the Commander-in-Chief, and explain the difficulties of the Mission. On 14 September, the Mission received a signal announcing the withdrawal of all cadre battalions from China to India.

The history of the 204 Military Mission to China is not glorious. No battles were won, no medals were awarded. They died of dirt and disease. They were ignorant and afraid. But if some were the scourings of the army, others were the pick. Underfed, ill-clothed and ill-equipped, they marched until they were barefooted. Sick, they staggered until they died. They did their duty.

THESE WERE TRULY THE FORGOTTEN MEN.

For the Allies, the war in Burma was over in May 1942; the time had arrived to plan its re-occupation. Initially, this began on a small scale in the Kachin area of northern Burma. This area was to the north of Myitkyina and was a triangle formed by the confluence of two rivers – the Mali Hka and the Nmai Hka. The Kachins were independent, hardworking, stockily-built hillmen. Many of them had become recruits of the Burma army and those fortunate to avoid capture returned to their hill villages. Their location brought them into little contact with the outside world and they lived happily with a minimum of British administration. It was this area of Burma to which the British directed their first re-occupation attention.

In July 1942, at the village of Putao, twelve armed British engineers were parachuted in equipped with picks and shovels. With the willing help of locals, a small landing strip was constructed and then a Hawker Audax trainer landed from which emerged a lean and freckled Australian, Lieutenant Colonel Gamble, representing the British Army, who had instructions to occupy Fort Hertz and commence operations against the Japanese. Then an RAF Dakota was flown in to evacuate the engineers and the pilot of the Audax trainer which had tipped on its nose on landing. Lieutenant Colonel Gamble was an ANZAC who had fought at Gallipoli in the 1914-18 war. Afterwards, he joined the Indian Army and subsequently transferred to the Burma Military Police, being stationed at Fort Hertz where he learnt about the Kachins, their habits and language, and made many friends. He received a very warm welcome from the local tribesmen who showed a strong desire to fight the Japanese intruders. Gamble selected twenty-four stalwarts from hundreds of volunteers and with twelve elephants, a few mules and ponies and half a dozen patriotic Chinese traders, set off down the ninety-five mile road to Sumprabum, a little less than half way to Myitkyina. He sent messengers ahead to spread the glad tidings amongst the Kachins and to let it be known that the Japanese must believe a large force was advancing on them. The Kachins did their work nobly and rumours soon reached the Japanese that a strong force, miles and miles in length, with armoured cars, jeeps and elephants, was advancing on Sumprabum. By the time Gamble reached the village on 10 September, the Japanese had pulled out and were retreating in all haste towards Myitkyina.

Leaving a few men to organise the Kachins round Sumprabum, Gamble set off after the Japanese, with Kachins flocking to his banner wherever he went. The number of men Gamble could recruit was strictly limited by the supply potential. Everything they needed would have to be flown in from India, resulting in hundreds of disappointed Kachins being turned away.

Gamble and his force followed the Japanese right down to within a few miles of Myitkyina. He had been ordered, first, to organise a body to be known as the Northern Kachin Levies, secondly, to obtain information about the Japanese, and, thirdly, to harass the enemy. The first had been quickly done, the second also, and it is doubtful if in any other theatre of war the Allies had such exact information on the enemy's movements as that supplied by those Kachin levies. They had their men freely travelling up and down the railway, working as interpreters for the Japanese, finding garrison and headquarter locations, plotting troop movements and learning of road-building projects. The difficulty lay in getting the information back to headquarters in India. Soon wireless sets were flown in and regular intelligence officers were on the job, collecting and passing on information and giving the RAF and USAAF bombing and strafing targets.

The third task of harassing the enemy was fulfilled with zeal and delight by the Kachins. That was just the warfare they understood: ambush, night marches through the jungle, surprise attacks. Many times the Japanese sent out patrols to wipe them out. The Kachins would hide in the jungle, set traps just off the trail with fire-hardened, needle sharp bamboo spikes or *panjis,* and when the Japanese were opposite their traps, fire from ten or twelve-feet range. Many Japanese who survived the first volleys would rush to the side of the trail, sometimes throwing themselves flat on the ground, catching their legs or impaling their bodies on the ferocious *panjis.* Time and time again this happened.

This form of harassment was a problem for the Japanese who obviously wanted to push up to and occupy Fort Hertz. The delaying tactics of the Kachins proved invaluable to the Allies who had decided that a road some 300 miles should be built from Ledo, the rail terminal in north-east India, to Mogaung, thirty miles south of Myitkyina on the main Mandalay-Myitkyina railway. By the end of 1942, with US Army involvement, the road was under way.

At the same time, the first offensive operation commenced against the Japanese in the Arakan, with Maungdaw and Buthidaung as the initial targets. The ultimate objective was the occupation of Akyab, where possession of the airfields would have enabled the RAF to provide air cover for subsequent operations against Rangoon.

So, as No. 27 Squadron was being re-formed with Beaufighters towards the end of 1942, the overall picture in Burma was as follows.

In the north-east along the Salween River, the Japanese were trying to break up Chinese concentrations.

In the north, the Japanese had started a big push against the Northern Kachin levies with the occupation of Fort Hertz as the objective.

Along the Hukawang Valley, the Japanese were massing to drive against the Chinese and the Americans building the Ledo Road.

In the north-west, the Naga Hills and the Chin Hills were being taken care of by the tribespeople with a steady build-up of regular soldiers as a counter to increasing penetration by the Japanese.

In the south at Arakan, the British and the Japanese were locked in a bitter struggle for the approaches to Akyab.

2 · NO. 27 SQUADRON
– BORN 1915

In the 1939-45 war there were permanent and specially formed wartime squadrons, the latter included Dominion Squadrons from Australia, Canada, New Zealand and South Africa. The wartime squadrons were quickly disbanded when hostilities ceased whereas the permanent squadrons reverted to their normal peacetime activities.

No. 27 Squadron was a permanent RAF squadron which had been formed at Hounslow, England, on 5 November 1915. It went to France in March 1916 and was engaged as a general reconnaissance squadron carrying out patrols and photographic reconnaissance, and it took part in the main operations from the Somme offensive onwards. During 1918, the squadron's duties were mainly confined to bombing, both in support of troops and on distant targets, and it was as a bomber squadron that it ended the 1914-1918 war. It returned to England in March 1919 and was disbanded at Shotwick shortly afterwards.

During this period, No. 27 squadron was first equipped with the Martinsyde G100 Scout, a two-seat biplane, powered by one 120 hp Beardmore engine; because of its shape, the aircraft was known as the 'Elephant', or 'Jumbo'. It was not long before an elephant insignia appeared on the fuselages of the squadron's aircraft, which led to the elephant becoming the centre-piece of the squadron's badge, which was officially authorised by King Edward VIII in 1936. The squadron adopted as its motto QUAM CELERRIME AD ASTRA (With All Speed To The Stars). In 1917, the squadron was re-equipped with the de Havilland DH4, a two-seat high-level bomber powered by one 200 hp engine and able to carry twice the bomb-load of the Martinsyde, two 230-pound bombs.

When hostilities ceased in November 1918, the squadron had lost about 150 aircrew and had been awarded very few decorations. In comparison, in the fifteen-month period from when No. 27 Squadron became operational with Beaufighters in December 1942 until it was withdrawn for operational rest in March 1944, thirty-two aircrew lost their lives and five decorations were awarded.

No. 27 Squadron was reformed in India on 1 April 1920 at Mianwali on the Indus, and was equipped with the de Havilland DH9As, a two-seat bomber. It arrived at the beginning of the Waziristan Campaign which had begun in 1919 and continued to 1925. For this campaign, No. 27 Squadron operated from various frontier stations and advanced landing grounds. In 1927, one flight operated from Miranshah in the campaign of that year against the Mohmands, the remainder of the squadron operating in support of Army columns from Peshawar.

In 1930, operations again took place on the North-West Frontier, which continued in 1931. In 1933, there was a short sharp campaign against the Mohmands. At the time, No. 27 Squadron was flying from Kohat. In 1935, trouble again broke out on the frontier and active operations, in which No. 27 Squadron took part, began in August. In January 1936, the squadron flew to Singapore and on its return to Kohat in February, found the campaign still in progress. It continued until April 1939. In 1939 and 1940 No. 27 Squadron was based at Risalpur as a flying training unit, forming the nucleus of the first Flying Training School for the Indian Air Force. It was equipped with Wapitis, Hawker Harts and DH Tiger Moths. In this period, the squadron received its mobilisation orders and split into three flights. Two flights were moved to Madras and Bombay on anti-submarine and shipping patrols.

It is interesting that a leave camp was established at Murree, some 6000 feet above the north-west plains, where members of the squadron obtained relief from the heat of the plains, because the same leave pattern became a part of No. 27 Squadron activities in 1943-44. The twenty years which No. 27 Squadron served in the North-West Frontier were to see it become associated with two other RAF squadrons, Nos 31 and 60. No. 31 Squadron was a transport unit which, since its formation late in 1915, had been based in that part of the world. No. 60 Squadron, like No. 27 Squadron, was a general purpose squadron.

Then, in January 1941, Blenheim Mk I bombers began to arrive for Nos 27 and 60 Squadrons and it was not long before a rumour was around that the roles of the two squadrons was once more to change. This proved to be true and, in February 1941, No. 27 Squadron received movement orders to transfer, as a Blenheim squadron, to Singapore – a flight occupying five days, including night stops at Cawnpore, Calcutta, Rangoon and Alor Star. A total of thirteen Blenheims made the journey to Singapore, with the ground staff being flown by 'A' Flight of No. 31 Squadron's Vickers Valentias and two British Overseas Airway's Armstrong Whitworth Atlantas. At the same time, No. 60 Squadron's Blenheims were ordered to Rangoon with the ground staff being flown in by 'B' Flight of No. 31 Squadron. All three squadrons – 27, 31 and 60 – subsequently became involved in the Burma Campaign, and shared Agartala aerodrome, East Bengal, for a period during 1943.

Throughout 1941, No. 27 Squadron was moved progressively north into Malaya, first to Butterworth in May and then in August to Sungei Patani, whilst at nearby Alor Star another RAF Blenheim squadron, No. 62, was based – they were the only short-nose Blenheim Mk Is in Malaya. After a visit to Singapore on 20 November, No. 27

Squadron's Commanding Officer, Squadron Leader F. R. C. Fowle, informed the aircrews that the Blenheims were to be replaced with Marylands or Beaufighters. However, with the entry of Japan into World War Two, these plans were never put into effect and instead, the squadron was virtually wiped out as an operational unit on day one of the campaign. The first Japanese attack against Malaya on 8 December occurred at approximately the same time as the attack on Pearl Harbor on 7 December – the dates differing because Hawaii and Malaya are on opposite sides of the international date line.

Sergeants Jack Woodward and Ron Winzar were RAAF observers and had joined No. 27 Squadron at Sungei Patani in November. Woodward was Duty Pilot from 8am on 7 December to 8am on 8 December. During the night of 7/8 December, word came through that the Japanese had bombed Singapore and had landed troops at Khota Bharu – Woodward was instructed by Squadron Leader Fowle to prepare the flare path for immediate use. Eight Blenheims took off at 6.45am for operations at Khota Bharu and almost immediately there were two Japanese raids of five bombers each on Sungei Patani, rendering the main landing strip unserviceable and putting out of action several Brewster Buffalo single engine fighters of No. 21 Squardon, RAAF which shared Sungei Patani with No. 27 Squadron, and was under the command of Squadron Leader Allshore. An emergency landing strip was quickly marked out, enabling the Blenheims which had been away for three hours to land safely, although several had been shot up and some of the aircrews injured. During the second bombing attack three Buffalos of No. 21 Squadron took off to engage the Japanese. However, mainly because of armament problems, they caused no damage to the Japanese bombers.

Late in the morning another raid, this time by twenty-seven Japanese bombers, took a severe toll of the Blenheims and the remaining Buffalos. One Blenheim, piloted by Sergeant Willows, took off as bombs were falling and flew over an exploding bomb which killed the crew instantly. After this raid, those aircraft that could still fly were sent down to Singapore and Butterworth. At Butterworth, they were to suffer more bombing and also strafing attacks before another evacuation was made on 15 December to Kuala Lumpur and Singapore.

The remaining weeks of the campaign were very confusing for all of the Allied forces in Malaya, Singapore, Sumatra and Java. No. 27 Squadron was no longer an independent squadron and what was left of it became a part of No. 225 Group, RAF. Sergeant Woodward was a Duty Pilot at Kallang aerodrome, Singapore, before it became time to fly any serviceable aircraft to Sumatra. This brought together the remnants of No. 27 and No. 62 Squadrons, both flying Blenheims, which then operated as No. 27 Squadron under Squadron Leader Banks from a little known emergency landing aerodrome called P2 some 40 miles from Palembang.

On the morning of 14 February, four of the Blenheims, including that of RAAF observer Sergeant Woodward, RAF pilot Warrant Officer Kennedy and RAAF wireless air gunner Sergeant Clarke, took off to look for a convoy of Japanese ships reported to comprise one cruiser, two destroyers and nine transports. The four aircraft became separated, and, suddenly, Sergeant Woodward's aircraft came across two convoys of fourteen and twenty-four transports with a naval escort of aircraft carriers, cruisers and destroyers. This turned out to be the Sumatra invasion fleet that landed at Palembang the next day. The four Blenheims made two bombing and strafing attacks on the invasion ships and barges at the entrance to the Musi River, Palembang, for the loss of one Blenheim. On landing after the second attack, the three crews found that practically all of the squadron personnel had left P2 by road for the southern tip of Sumatra hoping to find a ship to take them across the Sunda Straits to Java. They were briefed to fly immediately to Batavia (now Jakarta), but, because of a severe Sumatra storm, Sergeant Woodward's aircraft ran out of fuel after finally crossing the Java coast where it was crash landed. The three aircrew caught up with the remnants of No. 27 Squadron at Kalijati where the total strength of all RAF Blenheims left in the campaign was six.

On 24 February, two Blenheims flew to Jogjakarta, Central Java, where it was believed spare parts were available. Sergeant Woodward's Blenheim had no sooner landed when a string of Japanese dive bombers, escorted by about eighteen Navy Zero fighters, destroyed three Allied aircraft and severely damaged the two Blenheims and aerodrome buildings. It could be said that No. 27's 'swan song' as a Blenheim squadron was at Jogjakarta on 24 February.

Two days later, Woodward and other Air Force personnel were taken by train to Tjilijap on the southern Java coast where they boarded the vessel *Khota Gehe* – one of a fifteen ship convoy which set sail for Fremantle, Western Australia, on 27 February. However, the convoy became a Battle of Sunda Straits target. The *Khota Gehe* was one of the few ships to survive, eventually reaching Colombo, Ceylon on 6 March.

Although No. 60 Squadron's base was Mingaladon aerodrome, Rangoon, a detachment of eight Blenheim Mk I with 100 personnel was sent to Kuantan, Malaya on 1 December 1941 for a six week armament practice exercise, leaving behind at Mingaladon the squadron's other four Blenheims.

Within one week of arriving at Kuantan the detachment found itself very much a part of the Japanese invasion of northern Malaya and southern Siam, becoming associated again with No. 27 Squadron, which was based at nearby Sungei Patani, in carrying out bombing raids against the enemy. The squadron suffered early aircraft losses, and, on 9 December, the remaining four Blenheims were evacuated to Tengah aerodrome, Singapore. On arrival, they were immediately briefed by a Group Captain Watson to supply three aircrews to join with three aircrews of No. 34 Squadron, making a flight of six Blenheim Mk IVs for a bombing raid that afternoon on Singora airfield in southern Siam. The aircrew of No. 60 Squadron had not previously flown the Blenheim Mk IVs. They were told that they might be joined over Butterworth by No. 62 Squadron Blenheim Mk IVs and No. 27 Squadron Blenheim Mk Is as fighter escort, but this did not happen because Butterworth was being bombed at the rendezvous time. They were also told that they should land at whatever aerodrome they could reach after the raid on Singora as they would not have sufficient fuel to return to Singapore.

One of the Blenheims, crewed by Sergeant Johnstone (pilot), Pilot Officer Kingwill (navigator) and Sergeant Gregory (wireless air gunner) of No. 60 Squadron, became separated from the formation over Singora and proceeded to bomb the Japanese invasion fleet, instead of Singora aerodrome. It was shot down by Japanese fighters and the three injured crew were picked up by the Japanese. They were tortured by their captors and, after spending three months in a Saigon prison, were transferred to Changi jail, Singapore, before moving to the infamous Burma/Siam railway. All three survived captivity. In the same raid, another No. 60 Squadron aircrew was lost when their Blenheim was shot down. Flight Sergeant Smith (navigator) and Sergeant Fowler (wireless air gunner), were killed, although it was later reported that the pilot, Flight Lieutenant Dobson, was captured but was beheaded by the Japanese.

Like No. 27 and most other squadrons, No. 60 had become a fragmented operational unit and, on 24 December, all personnel were shipped to Rangoon on the S.S. *Darvel* and the M.V. *Hermelin*. They arrived in Rangoon at the end of the month to re-join their base unit of four Blenheims at Mingaladon and to become immediately involved in the Burma campaign.

So the era of No. 27 Squadron equipped with the Beaufighter arrived. But first, about the Beaufighter.

It was a product of the Bristol Aeroplane Co. Ltd., Bristol, England. It was designed in 1938 as a variant of the Beaufort, Bristol Type 152, and first flew in July 1939. An all-metal aircraft weighing about ten tons, it was extremely robust and was able to withstand physical damage to a considerable degree, as evidenced during the Burma Campaign.

The production versions built in England during World War Two were the Marks I, II, VI, X and XI. All marks of Beaufighter were powered by two Bristol Hercules air-cooled, sleeve-valve radial engines, except the Mark II, which was fitted with Rolls-Royce Merlin inline liquid-cooled engines, an experiment at a time when the Hercules was in great demand for heavy bomber production. However, the handling and performance were not up to requirements and it was quickly scrapped.

The Mark I with its flat tailplane was very light on the controls and in Britain was a beautiful aircraft to fly. However, the lack of longitudinal stability made the aircraft tiring to fly on instruments. To counteract this lightness and thus provide the pilot with improved longitudinal stability, the tailplane of later models was modified to have twelve degree dihedral. No. 27 Squadron was equipped with Marks VI, X and XI at various times of its activities in Burma and most of the aircraft had the dihedral tailplane. The Mark VI had two 1600 hp Hercules, and the Marks X and XI had two

1735 hp Hercules. Because of their engines' silence, the Beaufighters earned the name 'Whispering Death', and on operations it was of tremendous advantage to come onto targets at tree-top level and gain the maximum element of surprise. Being air-cooled, the Hercules' big disadvantage in hot climates was the short time that they took to heat up on the ground – if the temperature reached 220 degrees Fahrenheit before take-off, it was recommended that they be shut down.

The Beaufighter did not have dual controls and initially it was not an easy aircraft to fly, especially for those of us who had not long received our Empire Air Training Scheme wings. My own initiation, and that of many of the original No. 27 Squadron Beaufighter pilots, was at No. 2(C) Operational Training Unit, Catfoss, East Yorkshire, England. We stood behind our instructor (in my case it was Flight Lieutenant Stubbs), watched what he did for a few take-offs and landings, then saw him climb out of the pilot's seat and say 'it's all yours'. I do not think I have ever felt so lonely as when he had gone, the hatch shut, and I was at the controls for the first time.

The Beaufighter was a very powerful aircraft, sometimes referred to as 'two large engines followed by an aeroplane', and going solo the first time was not deemed wise on the Catfoss runways. Instead, we were taken to nearby Driffield airfield which was a very large all-grass aerodrome. Here you could open up the engines, get the feel of the power and the swing they generated, and by a quick assessment of what to do – in particular, get the tail up – suddenly find yourself in the air and half-way across England. The Beaufighter was claimed to be the fastest aircraft of its class in the world at sea level, a feature the aircrews of No. 27 Squadron greatly appreciated when confronted with the Japanese single-engine fighters, for there was no way we could mix it with the Zeros in aerial combat – our greatest asset when confronted with the Japanese fighters was the speed of the Beaufighter at ground level. In India/Burma we cruised at 170/175 knots at 1800 rpm and − 2 pounds boost, but by increasing the revs and boost to 2600 and + 6, the speed would reach 280 knots straight and level.

As might be expected, after they learned of the procedure the new pilots went through to go solo, the new incoming navigators to Catfoss had some reservations about the ability of their prospective future pilots to handle the Beaufighter.

One day we watched a strange Beaufighter land at Catfoss and to our surprise out climbed an attractive female pilot, who, as a member of the Air Transport Auxiliary, had ferried this new aircraft from the factory to Catfoss. This prompted one of the navigators to remark, 'Look, a girl – they can't be that difficult to fly'. It was as a member of this valuable wartime Air Transport Auxiliary that famous pre-war aviatrix, Amy Johnson, lost her life.

With my wife, I revisited Catfoss and Driffield in 1977. At that time there was a caravan factory on the aerodrome and the runway was in use to store caravans. Driffield had been turned into a training school for army transport drivers and the aerodrome looked like an obstacle course. But the visit did bring back memories.

Another feature of the Beaufighter was its heavy armament – four 20 mm Hispano cannons and six 0.303-inch (7.7 mm) Browning machine guns, the cannon trajectory being set at seven degrees to provide for low level attacks at 700 yards. All the guns were fixed and fired forward, activated by the pilot pulling a trigger for the cannons and pushing a button for the machine guns. The trigger and button were on the control column and when fired simultaneously reduced the speed of the aircraft by some 10 knots. With a magazine of 250 rounds for each Hispano and 1,000 for each Browning, there was enough ammunition to allow usually ten generous attacks to be made on each operation. There was provision for a rear-firing machine gun in the navigator's position but it was not a success in Burma, whereas in the Western Desert, where enemy aircraft were more prevalent, it did provide the navigators with a degree of security. Its disadvantages were that it took up much of the navigator's space and allowed cold air to enter the aircraft through the slot in the canopy. It was mainly a 'scare' gun but because of the Beaufighter's speed it was not of any real value and it soon ceased to be a feature of the Beaufighter in Burma.

The fuselage cannon and wing machine gun ports were covered with canvas patches to prevent debris and humidity causing the guns to malfunction. Once the canvas was broken after the first firing, the ports created a whistle effect which could be heard from the ground and so when an aircraft was in the landing circuit after an operation it was easy to tell whether or not the cannons and/or machine guns had been fired.

The effect of firing the cannons and machine guns on the aircraft compasses was considerable, throwing them out by as much as forty to fifty degrees. On operations in Burma it was standard practice after completing attacks on the target to fly on a south to north course for a short time, firing a burst of cannon/machine gun which had the effect of bringing the compass back to a true reading. Sometimes this was not successful and so it became necessary to swing the aircraft compass, which could take up to half a day, before the aircraft went out again on operations.

There is no doubt that the pilots and their navigators who flew Beaufighters on operations found them to be magnificent aircraft, one that gave tremendous confidence and a sense of pride in the knowledge that it was a very lethal weapon that could inflict much damage to the enemy. It was used for a wide range of attack operations, including torpedo dropping. In Burma it was mainly used as a long-range low-level attack aircraft against Japanese lines of communication, including railways, roads, rivers, aerodromes and troop concentrations, up to 500 miles from base.

I had one reservation about the Beaufighter's design for the pilot's comfort, and nothing could be done to avoid it without jeopardising his life should he have to ditch in the ocean. The pilot's seat was the traditional fighter bucket type, meaning that he sat on his parachute for the duration of each operation, which in Burma averaged four and a half hours. Part of the parachute assembly was the dinghy pack which included a CO_2 bottle to inflate the dinghy should a forced landing in the ocean be necessary. After being strapped in for a few hours, this bottle became rather uncomfortable because of its pressure on the pilot's bottom, but it was a small price to pay if one day a pilot found himself in the ocean without an aircraft – fortunately, this did not happen to me. Adding to the pilot's discomfort when flying on operations were the money belt, revolver and knife around his waist, which we all carried in case of a forced landing in, or having to parachute into, enemy territory.

The author's wings parade at No. 7 SFTS, Fort Macleod, Canada, in November 1941. The author is fourth from the left in the front row. From No. 7 SFTS, the author went to No. 2(C) OTU in the United Kingdom.

The author on No. 31 General Reconnaissance Course at Prince Edward Island, Canada in December 1941. Canada was a major training area under the Empire Air Training Scheme.

Magwe aerodrome. Top: 21 March 1942 was a black day for No. 45 (Blenheim) Squadron, RAF, sustained twenty-four hour bombing by Japanese aircraft destroying the squadron as an operational unit. Bottom: Remnants of No. 45 Squadron withdrawing from Burma after the Magwe raids.

Fort Hertz, 1942. Top: Re-establishing air supply lines to the Kachin levies by Dakotas. Bottom: The traditional means of supplying the Kachin levies after the Japanese occupation of Burma.

Jack Woodward (observer), Jock Kennedy (pilot) and 'Clicker' Clarke (wireless air gunner) alongside their crashed Blenheim at Java on 15 February 1942 after evacuating from Palembang, Sumatra.

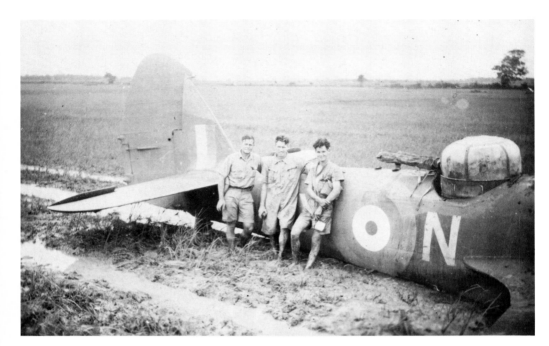

Aircrew at Kalijati, Java, in February 1942. Three were members of No. 27 Squadron – from the left, Flight Lieutenant Kentish, second from the left, Sergeant Woodward and fifth from the left, Flight Lieutenant Dunn.

On board the *Khota Gede*. Two meals a day were served between Tjilijap, Southern Java and Colombo, Ceylon.

Top: A Beaufighter Mk IF over England, and, above, a Mark VIF at Agartala, India.

No. 16 (Pilots) Course, No. 2(C) Operational Training Unit, Catfoss, England, in May 1942. The author is fourth from the left in the front row.

Some of the original aircrew postings to No. 27 Squadron in Cairo, Egypt in November 1942. Back row: Pilot Officers Ginger Hassall, Jerry Goodman, Edgar Welch, Sandy Dinwoodie and Ken Herbert. Front row: Flying Officer Reg Williams, author, Pilot Officer Paddy Sterling.

The first commanding officer, Wing Commander Harry Daish, an Australian serving with the RAF in England when World War Two started.

The CO's navigator, Flight Lieutenant Frankie Franklin, DFC.

The Officers mess at Amarda Road at Christmas 1942. The dog, Tiki, belonged to Flight Lieutenant Snow Swift. On the mess wall above the fireplace was a large squadron badge, the work of Flight Sergeant George Salter, 'B' Flight engineer.

Ground party crossing the
Brahmaputra River on the way
from the RAF Maintenance Unit
at Kanchrapara to Agartala, the
capital of Tripura State in what is
now Bangladesh, in January
1943.

How the Officers compound at Agartala looked under monsoon conditions.

The Officers basha hut accommodation at Agartala.

The Officers mess and kitchen at Agartala.

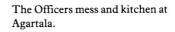

'B' Flight get together at Agartala in 1943: aircrew on the wings of a Beaufighter and their groundcrew.

'B' Flight aircrew, in 1943, en route to the Agartala airstrip in the Flight gharrie, with the Flight's second commander, Squadron Leader Birt, behind the driving wheel.

'A' Flight aircrew in 1943, with Flight Commander Bunny Horne at the left end of the rear row.

Bengali children in the Officers compound at Agartala.

The author at Agartala beside his Beaufighter, in 1943.

The author and Pilot Officer Nobby Clark discussing a maintenance problem at Agartala in 1943.

The author taking-off, below, and, bottom, landing at Agartala in 1943.

The author's team at the Air Fighting Training Unit at Amarda Road in 1943: Fitter Corporal Sammy Cohen, centre, and navigator Pilot Officer Paddy Sterling, right.

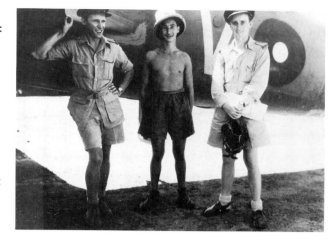

Organising a 'bucket brigade' to put out the Officers mess fire at Amarda Road. On the left, hands on hips, is Wing Commander Daish.

The Lushai Hills which separated India from Burma, and typical of the mountains over which most sorties were flown.

A typical monsoon sky, Agartala, 1943, with a Beaufighter in the foreground undergoing post-mission servicing.

3 · REFORMING '27' – 1942

The decision to reform No. 27 Squadron on Beaufighters for operational flying in Burma was announced in September 1942. It was the first unit to be equipped with Beaufighters in the Far East and was to be the first of three squadrons that would make up a Beaufighter Wing to operate in the Burma theatre of war. The squadron records state:

19th September, 1942. No. 27 Squadron formed. Authority Formation Order No. 287 issued by Air Headquarters, India, dated the 3rd December, 1942, reference 3116/311/Org. The squadron's establishment will be India/703 when the Government of India's sanction has been obtained. The squadron will be under the direct control of No. 224 Group.

On 23 September, four officers, together with 320 airmen, arrived at the RAF station at Armada Road in the State of Orissa, approximately 130 miles south-west of Calcutta, on the way to Madras. There were two flying officers, G. M. Hamilton, the Intelligence Officer, and R. G. Campbell, the Medical Officer (who was subsequently replaced on 8 February 1943, by his namesake, Flight Lieutenant Campbell, a very likeable Scotsman), and two pilot officers, J. M. Brewer, the Technical (Engineer) Officer, and J. M. Talbot, the A&SD (Adjutant). They were followed in November by Flying Officer G. McBride, the A&SD (Defence), an Australian in the RAF, and Pilot Officer A. L. Farthing, the Equipment Officer.

So far the squadron was without aircraft, aircrew or a Commanding Officer, but not for long, although there was some administration confusion about the posting of Wing Commander H. C. Daish, an Australian in the RAF, as the squadron's first Commanding Officer. He had left the United Kingdom by ship in August 1942, accompanied by a number of Beaufighter aircrews with the intention of picking up Beaufighters at Takoradi on the west coast of Africa and flying them to the Middle East. However, this did not happen, and the aircrews were eventually flown in small groups from West Africa to Cairo where they were quickly given postings to Middle East squadrons.

Air Headquarters, Middle East, knew nothing of the Air Ministry plans for Wing Commander Daish to be the CO of the new No. 27 Squadron in India, and proceeded to find him a suitable posting. It was only when the Air Ministry, London, were notified by Air Headquarters, Middle East, that Wing Commander Daish had been posted as Commanding Officer to form No. 454 Squadron, an Australian light bomber unit, and proceed to Teheran, Persia (now Iran), that he learnt that he was supposed to be in India reforming No. 27 squadron. As he said, 'Pity someone in the UK didn't tell me before I left'. As a result of this confusion Wing Commander Daish eventually reached No. 27 Squadron at Amarda Road on 3 December. He had been able to team up with his previous navigator, Pilot Officer Franklin, with whom he had flown on No. 235 Squadron in the UK.

Aircrew postings had been made that included seven crews from Middle East RAF Beaufighter squadrons, Nos 227, 252 and 272, stationed at Edku and Luqa. The remaining postings were crews arriving from the UK, mostly from No. 2(C) OTU, Catfoss. The foundation crews (RAF unless otherwise stated), in order of arrival at Amarda Road and Kanchrapara, comprised: 18 November 1942: Flight Lieutenant R. A. Swift, RAAF and Pilot Officer L. A. Clark; Flight Sergeant J. S. France, RNZAF, and Sergeant Noble; 22 November 1942: Sergeant K. A. Graham and Warrant Officer L. J. Powdrill; 3 December 1942: Wing Commander H. C. Daish and Pilot Officer W. M. Franklin; 4 December 1942: Flying Officer E. B. Horn and Warrant Officer J. Blake; Pilot Officer S. C. Laing, RCAF and Pilot Officer W. M. House; Pilot Officer J. L. Mason, RCAF and Sergeant Dunbar; 9 December 1942: Sergeant B. J. Hartness and Sergeant J. A. Shortis; 13 December 1942: Pilot Officer J. Cotter and Sergeant H. F. Cooper; Sergeant K. H. Spratt and Sergeant H. Adcroft; 17 December 1942: Pilot Officer P. A. S. Thompson and Pilot Officer K. M. Merritt; Pilot Officer J. D. Hassell and Pilot Officer G. Goodman; Sergeant C. G. Johnson and Pilot Officer A. M. Dinwoodie; Pilot Officer J. Townsend and Pilot Officer K. Wandless; 12 January 1943: Pilot Officer D. J. Innes, RAAF and Pilot Officer R. A. Sterling; 27 January 1943: Squadron Leader P. F. Illingworth, DFC, and Sergeant Osguthorpe; Flying Officer R. R. Williams and Pilot Officer K. E. Herbert; Sergeant R. D. Thorogood and Pilot Officer E. S. Welch.

With the exception of Wing Commander Daish, who was a permanent RAF Officer, all of the original No. 27 Squadron aircrew were 'wartime' airmen. For them to come together with a minimum of war experience and develop into a very successful operational squadron was perhaps indicative of the spirit that prevailed among young men in those days who joined up to do a job for their country.

The traditional route for aircraft flying from the Middle East to India – Service and civil – was the 'oil pipeline route'. The first three crews, Flight Lieutenant Swift, Flight Sergeant France and Sergeant Graham, with their navigators Pilot Officer Clark, Sergeant Noble, and Warrant Officer Powdrill, flew this route, and aircraft T5208, flown by Swift, was the first Beaufighter to land on Indian soil, on 5 November 1942.

It was on 23 October, that Swift, then a pilot officer with No. 272 (Beaufighter) Squadron, RAF, at Edku near Alexandria, after returning from a successful attack on German transports in the Libyan desert, was informed of his promotion to flight lieutenant and immediate posting to No. 27 Squadron, India, as flight commander of 'B' Flight. His 'personal gear' for the flight to India included his dog, Tickton (which he promoted from Air Vice Desert Dog to Air Rajah Dog), a portable gramophone and ballet records.

On 27 October, the three aircraft took off from L.G. 224 (West Cairo) aerodrome for Habbaniya in Iraq with a brief 'if conditions get bad in the Syrian desert try to find the oil pipeline and follow it to Baghdad'.

First, Swift's aircraft developed engine trouble and all three aircraft returned to L.G. 224. On the second attempt, Flight Sergeant France's entrance hatch blew open and again they returned to L.G. 224. Their next attempt was not until 1 November, when they reached Habbaniya, after being forced to use the oil pipeline for a short period because of a severe dust storm.

Habbaniya was a permanent RAF station, with facilities such as a swimming pool. After a thorough check of the three aircraft, followed by air tests, they were cleared for India on 4 November. Flight Sergeant France could not resist the temptation to beat up the control tower and found himself on the mat when he reached India. The next stage was to Sharja, near Dubai, a five-hour flight down the Arabian Gulf.

After an overnight stop they took off for Karachi, but after two hours flying Sergeant Graham's aircraft developed engine trouble and he called the other aircraft to say he did not like his chances of reaching Karachi. They had been briefed about an emergency landing strip at Jiwani, Baluchistan, and promptly headed for it to find an isolated strip on top of a barren escarpment where he had to be left to the tender mercy of a rather primitive RAF set-up. The other two aircraft continued on to Karachi which they reached after some difference of opinion between Flight Lieutenant Swift and his navigator, Pilot Officer Clark, as to which course to fly. Prior to being posted to No. 2(C) OTU, Catfoss, all navigators and pilots did a two-months General Reconnaissance (GR) Course, which entailed a great deal of dead reckoning navigation over the sea. Thus Beaufighter pilots had very good training experience in navigating over water and, naturally, applied this training when the occasion arose. On this occasion, Swift was convinced that Clark's course would take them well south of Karachi – and he was right. There was a verbal showdown at Karachi but this was soon forgotten with their first beer on Indian (now Pakistani) soil.

Another service and air test of the two aircraft occupied four days during which time Sergeant Graham arrived, but again he was grounded for further maintenance to his aircraft when it became time to take off on 10 November. On this leg of the journey the two aircraft were directed to land at the private airfield of the Rajah of Jodhpur to enable him to inspect the Beaufighters! Again, more engine trouble – this time to Swift's aircraft whilst taxiing out to take off, resulting in an overnight stop. It was during this enforced stop that a signal came through from Group directing the aircraft to Calcutta instead of to Amarda Road where the squadron was forming. At Calcutta they would be required to carry out a flying demonstration for top RAF officers, including the AOC Bengal, Air Vice Marshal Williams, OBE, MC, DFC, and the Senior Air Staff Officer, Air Headquarters, Delhi.

By now only one of the three Beaufighters that had left Cairo on 1 November was serviceable and Swift continued with it to Calcutta after spending a night at Allahabad. The demonstration flight was made on 16 November and on 18 November, with Flight Sergeant France piloting one of the other aircraft, they reached Amarda Road. The actual flying time from Cairo to Amarda Road was 20 hours 25 minutes, although they had been "on the way" for 18 days. Their arrival signalled that the reformation of No. 27 Squadron as a Beaufighter squadron was under way. The squadron Adjutant, Pilot Officer, Talbot, informed Flight Lieutenant Swift that he was the most senior officer and would therefore be in command until the arrival of Wing Commander Daish in about two weeks time.

As Wing Commander Daish was about to take off from L.G. 224 (West Cairo) on the morning of 19 November, he was recalled to report to AHQME. Someone at No. 216 Group, Cairo, knew that he had experience in survey work and they decided to use him to survey a new route to India to determine if it would be a feasible alternative to the 'oil pipeline' route. The traditional route was becoming vulnerable to a German advance to the Suez Canal, or to a German advance through the Caucasus to Persia (now Iran).

At the time, 1942, Wadi Seidna near Khartoum in the Sudan was a very large aircraft pool for the Middle East, the aircraft being flown from the UK or from Takoradi on the West African coast. No. 216 Group, Cairo, wished to establish that aircraft for India – in particular Beaufighters – could be flown from Wadi Seidna to Karachi via Aden and Masira Island for overnight stops and that the servicing facilities were adequate. If so, it would save time and be much safer. The survey was generally successful and resulted in many aircraft for No. 27 and other squadrons using this route to reach India.

In my case, we flew from Wadi Seidna to Aden on 9 December, and the next morning took off for Masira Island, off the coast of Oman, with a refuelling stop at Salalah. As my navigator, Paddy Sterling, and I were boarding our Beau at Sheikh Othman aerodrome, Aden, an ammunition box was being loaded. On enquiry it turned out to be filled with bullion and was to be handed over at Salalah 'otherwise you won't be refuelled'! We could only assume that the right for RAF aircraft to refuel was at a price acceptable to the local Arabs! Without being able to refuel at Salalah, it would not have been possible to reach Masira Island, a fact of which the Arabs would be well aware in fixing a 'refuelling fee'. History has disclosed that what we were experiencing was only 'custom of the trade' so to speak. The then Sultan of Oman apparently approved most business related activities which, in 1942, included aircraft movements through Oman. Furthermore, he would only accept payment in Marie Theresa dollars.

After we took off from Aden I said to Paddy, 'Do you still want to stay in the war, or would you prefer to head south for East Africa, as I'm sure there's enough in that box to take care of our needs for the next few years.' We settled for the war.

Masira Island was plagued with flies and, after a service, it was a relief to take off next morning for Karachi. The aerodrome at Karachi, known as Drig Road, was the Indian terminal of the UK-India airship service. It had a very tall mooring mast and a huge hangar for the airship. However, the era of airship travel had not been the success anticipated – probably because of a couple of bad crashes – and these installations were basically redundant.

It was at this stage that some of the aircraft flying the Aden – Masira Island route developed mechanical problems. It was in the same general area that aircraft of Flight Lieutenant Swift's section, which had passed through earlier via the 'oil pipeline' route, also had mechanical problems – maybe the Beaus did not like the idea of finishing their service careers in India/Burma.

One aircraft burst its tailwheel at Masira Island. Wing Commander Daish flew on to Karachi hoping to pick up a spare tailwheel, and although there was not a Beaufighter tailwheel available – in fact, at the time there were no Beaufighter spare parts in India – he located a Beaufort tailwheel which would serve the purpose and flew it back to the grounded aircraft at Masira Island. Another aircraft, piloted by Pilot Officer Cotter, landed at Karachi with an oil pressure problem and was delayed for several days. On 15 December, after taking off from Drig Road for Jodhpur in company with Pilot Officer Thompson's Beaufighter, my aircraft developed undercarriage trouble to the extent that it would not lock in the retracted position. After flying in the direction of Jodhpur for forty-five minutes and not being able to rectify the problem, I returned to Drig Road. On inspection it was determined that replacement parts would have to be flown in from Habbaniya, Iraq, resulting in a frustrating three-week delay.

After Karachi, stops were made at Jodhpur and Allahabad, from where the final leg was flown to Amarda Road, an elapsed time from Wadi Seidna in the Sudan to Amarda Road of 21.35 flying hours over five days for aircraft that did not encounter mechanical problems.

With the acquisition of several aircraft, there developed an expectancy that operations would soon begin. However, before this was to happen there was a nasty fire on 17 December which started in the walkway between the officers' mess and the galley, resulting in the complete destruction of the galley and the Christmas goodies. Flight Lieutenant Swift was found responsible and had his pay-book docked. He was filling a petrol pressure lamp on a table at the other end of which he had set up a kerosene hurricane lamp and when he began to pour the petrol, which was aircraft fuel, a sheet of flame exploded between the two lamps – a distance of ten feet. He dropped the can and ran in flames for the compound where he was rolled in the dust to put out the flames. The fire spread to the galley, but fortunately a bucket brigade and the fire-tender saved the mess.

Although Flight Lieutenant Swift was not very popular all was forgiven on Christmas Day when in traditional style the officers and senior NCO's waited on the airmen in an atmosphere of great conviviality, but not before the squadron had made its first, albeit not very successful, operation against the Japanese.

4·AMARDA ROAD, KANCHRAPARA, AGARTALA – 1942/44

On 23 December the CO was summoned to a conference at No. 221 Group, Calcutta, and returned the same evening with the news that the first operation against the Japanese was to be made on the 25th, Christmas Day.

He took off the next day in command of five Beaufighters, first to Dum Dum aerodrome, Calcutta, for a briefing, then to Fenni aerodrome, East Bengal, from where, after an overnight stop, the operation was to be made. One aircraft, crewed by Flight Sergeant France and Sergeant Noble, had an accident on landing at Dum Dum and another, crewed by Pilot Officers Thompson and Merritt, developed engine trouble at Fenni.

So on Christmas Day 1942, exactly twelve months after the Japanese had begun their bombing of Rangoon, the first Beaufighter operation against the Japanese in Burma was carried out. The target was Toungoo aerodrome in central Burma which was being used by the Japanese to mount bombing raids on Arakan positions and Calcutta. Damage was done to three Japanese aircraft on the aerodrome before the Beaufighters' cannons jammed, causing the attacks to be aborted. The aircraft returned to Amarda Road.

Two days later, on 27 December, the second operation got under way, comprising four aircraft led by Flight Lieutenant Swift. They flew across the Bay of Bengal to Fenni aerodrome, from where the first operation had been made and from where they were to carry out the second operation the next day. The 27th was a Sunday and after three of the aircraft arrived – the fourth having returned to Amarda Road because of engine trouble – the crews attended a church service. In the afternoon the crews were briefed for a low-level attack on He-Ho aerodrome in the Southern Shan States of Eastern Burma. Early next morning they set course for He-Ho and as they descended into Burma for the first time they were struck by the colour of the Burmese foliage – the red and orange tints of the flowering trees which, in due course, we learnt to identify as the flame trees of the forest and the golden mohurs.

On reaching He-Ho aerodrome two of the Beaufighters went in to attack ground targets and Swift attacked a Japanese Mitsubishi Ki-21 (Type 97) bomber which was preparing to land. As with the first operation a few days earlier there were armament problems and on this occasion not a single gun fired! The Beaufighters returned to Fenni and were immediately redirected to Dum Dum aerodrome, Calcutta, where Group Intelligence Officers were waiting to interrogate them – in particular to discuss the armament problem.

The armament malfunction was a setback to Group's plans for the squadron to carry out regular attacks against the Japanese. Hurried meetings were held with No. 221 Group, culminating in visits by Wing Commander Buchanan, Senior Armament Officer, AHQ Delhi, and Flight Lieutenant Bourne, AHQ Bengal Engineering, to examine the Beaufighters' armament.

The result was a decision to move the squadron to the RAF Maintenance Unit at Kanchrapara, thirty miles north of Calcutta. Kanchrapara, which had an aerodrome, was a major Indian Railway workshop centre where engineering facilities were available to the RAF. Without further delay an advance party of two officers, two senior NCOs and nine other ranks left Amarda Road for Kanchrapara. The Technical advance party of one officer and nineteen other ranks followed on 8 January and the next day the squadron adjutant, Pilot Officer Talbot, in charge of five officers, 234 other ranks and eighteen followers, entrained.

The air party moved on 9 January and by the next day the entire squadron had reached Kanchrapara and then began the task of rectifying the armament problem. The problem was quickly identified as 'too much tension on some cannon links', which had the effect of preventing a cannon shell from releasing from its link when it reached the cannon breach.

The excessive tension turned out to be caused by slightly oversize cannon shells and meant that every cannon in the armory had to be individually tested for linkage tension. The squadron engineers devised how the testing should be carried out, and the somewhat frustrated aircrews did the testing. The testing method was simple. Sections of the cannon belt were suspended between two fixed posts with the cannon shells facing downwards. A metal weight was attached over the rim at the end of each shell. The weight was equivalent to the force required to allow the cannon shell to release from the link when the trigger was activated by the pilot. If the cannon shell separated from its link, it was passed; if not, it was discarded.

It was a slow and tedious job and as the 'passed' cannons were re-belted they were loaded back into the aircraft and then air-tested at the Hoglabada Air Firing Range in the delta area of the mouths of the Ganges River.

This was a really testing time for the squadron morale, and there was evidence that both ground and air crews were getting browned off. Not only had the cannon problem to be rectified and the guns air-tested, but it resulted in repetitive harmonization and calibration of each aircraft, which meant each had to be put up on blocks twice, requiring the manpower of the whole flight. After the tests were passed, the aircrew then had to swing the compasses of each aircraft. Another problem had developed, this time with the spark plugs, and, as a result, the Engineer Officer, Pilot Officer Brewer, was having his time fully occupied – eventually all spark plugs were replaced with another type.

To help the morale problem, a forty-eight hour leave system was introduced, followed by more frequent half-days off, which was supported by a 'liberty bus' into Calcutta (one and a half hour's drive) every afternoon at 13.30 hours, returning at 23.30 hours.

Coincidentally, from late December the Japanese commenced the night bombing of Calcutta, but there were no night-fighter aircraft in India to challenge the attacks. Some twenty-three bombing raids were made on Calcutta and, whilst the damage to military targets such as the Alipore docks was minimal, the effect on the local population was devastating. It was estimated that one and a half million fled the city. One local newsreel showed a bomb crater with the comment 'and so Calcutta takes its place beside London, Coventry, Malta'.

On visits to Calcutta during January with a uniform signifying we were pilots, it was very evident that the Bengalis did not think much of our capabilities as pilots in allowing this to happen. They were, in fact, quite forthright in their comments and attitudes, especially in places where we tended to congregate, such as Firpos Restaurant, The Grand Hotel, The Great Eastern Hotel, the '300' and the Saturday Clubs.

With most of the city cleaners gone, rubbish quickly accumulated and Calcutta became a serious plague centre. The AOC India, Air Chief Marshal Sir Richard Peirse, KCB, DSO, AFC, sought from Allied Command a section of night-fighters which were immediately provided in the form of three night-fighter Beaufighters from the Middle East. They were based on Dum Dum aerodrome at Calcutta and were immediately successful in halting the Japanese night raids.

On the first occasion, 15 January, Flight Sergeant Pring intercepted three bombers and shot all of them down within four minutes. Many Bengalis responded by returning to the city. The local newspapers carried the headlines 'PRING PRANGS THREE'. Four nights later, on 19 January, Flying Officer Crombie, an Australian pilot, intercepted four bombers and shot down two and possibly a third. However, during the engagement Crombie's aircraft was hit, causing an engine fire and blowing away the side perspex of his cockpit canopy resulting in both pilot and navigator baling out into the swamps of the Hooghly River and having to walk for three hours in chest deep water before reaching dry land. Pring and Crombie were immediately decorated with the DFM and DSO respectively. Both were subsequently killed in flying accidents – in the case of Crombie, it was in August 1945, after he had returned to Australia and was the Chief Flying Instructor (Squadron Leader, DSO, DFC) at No. 5 OTU, Williamtown.

That finished the Japanese night bombing of Calcutta. The Bengalis returned and

Calcutta became its old self once more. An extract from my navigator Paddy's diary of 22 January reads: 'Paid first visit to Calcutta with Bill, Tommy and Dave. Not impressed but had a lot of fun touring the low quarters, etc. Tommy has started to smoke and drink'. It was Paddy's 21st birthday on 18 January, and a special dinner was served in the Mess as he was the baby of the aircrew. Coincidentally, it was also my birthday.

It was whilst the cannon problem was being sorted out at Kanchrapara that the CO, Wing Commander Daish, was able to have a prototype camera mounting made that subsequently became a standard modification on all of the squadron aircraft. Wing Commander Daish's camera background went back to the early days of the original Photographic Reconnaissance Unit (PRU) at Heston, UK, at the beginning of 1940. There he was involved with the installation of the F24 camera in the wings of Spitfires for general reconnaissance over Europe.

The prototype mounting consisted of a bracket bolted to the half-inch armour plate situated immediately in front of the pilot. An F24 camera with a five-inch lens, normally used for vertical aerial photography, was then attached to the bracket so that the lens was facing forward and could take pictures of low-level attacks on Japanese targets. The camera was encased by the aircraft's nose fairing which was modified to have a perspex centre piece to accommodate the camera lens. The pilot operated the camera by a trigger on the control column. In practice, this meant that the pilot lined up his target, decided whether to fire 20 mm cannons or 0.303-in bullets, or both, and whether to take pictures. If he chose both cannons and bullets, this required the pushing by thumb of the machine gun button situated on the left side of the control column, pulling by right index finger the cannon trigger on the right side of the control column, and, if photographs were to be taken, pulling the camera trigger with his left index finger. Of course, he had the job of flying the aircraft into the right position to make the attack. In the target area the pilot really did not have time to relax and enjoy the scenery! But this extra flying duty often provided valuable enemy activity information to Allied intelligence. From one attack which I carried out in Central Burma on a train at Kume Road, Allied Intelligence was able to deduce that it was a special military train probably carrying an infantry battalion of 740 Japanese, stores and equipment and four tankettes. Whenever we landed from operations top priority was given to removing the camera and rushing it to Wing's Photographic Section for urgent developing.

The officers had been made members of the Kanchrapara Railway Officers Club where a cocktail party to make us feel at home was held on Saturday night, 30 January. The evening was going along smoothly until I, sitting at the bar between Snow Swift and John Cotter, accidentally knocked over John's drink. John's reaction was 'I don't like that', and Snow's response was to challenge John to fisticuffs – they had not been friendly towards each other at any time since we came together. Maybe it was because one was Irish and the other Australian, but something like this was probably bound to happen sooner or later. So outside, with me, unwittingly the cause of it all, holding a torch for them to see, to slog away at each other until the CO intervened, sending us all back to camp and informing us the next morning that we were banned from the Club. No doubt we were the shortest term members the Club ever had.

By 31 January, the squadron was able to declare six aircraft operationally serviceable and on 5 February advice was received from Group that we were to move immediately to Agartala, East Bengal, which was to become our operational base for the next year. A new sense of excitement and enthusiasm prevailed throughout the squadron.

The move to Agartala, as with the previous move from Amarda Road, was carried out in stages. On 7 February, a party of one senior NCO and five other ranks left with the largest of the squadron's motor transport units for Agartala by the sea route. This meant being shipped from Calcutta to Chittagong and then being driven about 150 miles north to Agartala.

On 8 February, the first air party moved. Eight aircraft, each with one ground crew, under Squadron Leader Illingworth, DFC, flew to Agartala to prepare for immediate operational flying. In a transport Hudson aircraft on the same day, the squadron intelligence officer, Flying Officer Wakelin, with a senior NCO and four other ranks,

The map is redrawn from a map of the airfield and location provided for aircrew in their flying notes. No. 27 Squadron occupied the area of the two dispersals and the hardstanding at the south-west of the airfield.

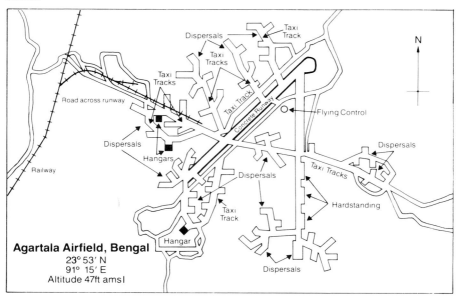

also made the move. The next day the second air party of six aircraft, again each with one ground crew, under Swift, flew to Agartala.

I was detailed to take one of the ground parties by train on the 9th, and the adjutant the remaining ground party on the 10th. The adjutant's party comprised three officers, ninety-two other ranks and thirty Indian other ranks, whilst my party comprised two officers and 164 other ranks. With the two parties were the squadron's stores, equipment and a number of transport vehicles. Much of the stores and equipment was loaded onto flat top rail wagons and strongly secured for the journey. Each party was, in fact, a special train and as events turned out, it was to be quite an adventure for my party.

My party left Kanchrapara mid-morning on 9 February and late in the afternoon, after travelling about 150 miles on the main north line to Darjeeling, reached the rail junction town of Parbatipur. We stayed there twenty-four hours, during which time we had to transfer all personnel and equipment to another train on the narrow gauge railway that would take us the rest of the way to Agartala. This leg of the journey was to include a crossing of the Brahmaputra River by special rail/river barges.

The accommodation on this narrow gauge train was not exactly first class! The small wooden carriages were in fact third class, dirty and alive with cockroaches and other creatures. There were loud protests which I conveyed to the rail authorities, only to be told there was nothing that could be done to improve the situation. This was not acceptable to the 164 other ranks who, having already spent one night on a very uncomfortable main line train, were not looking forward to another two nights on this narrow gauge line train.

The British have a knack for meeting difficult situations when they arise, and this was a challenge to their ingenuity.

It so happened that in a rail siding at Parbatipur was a set of coaches that made up the Chief Medical Officer of Bengal's medical train which attracted the attention of the men. By the time we were ready to leave late in the afternoon of the 10th, several leather cushions had apparently changed trains and although I did not see them I received a visit from two Army SPs demanding the return of the cushions, setting 6 pm as the deadline. When 6 o'clock arrived and the cushions were not returned, the SPs returned to search the train but without success, and so we departed leaving behind two angry SPs. The next morning on arrival at Bahadurbad Ghat on the Brahmaputra River, I learnt that the cushions were in fact on the train and had made the night's journey a little more comfortable for some than would otherwise have been the case. During the search at Parbatipur the cushions were hidden adjacent to our train and as the search was being carried out the cushions were being put back onto that section of the train already searched.

The sequel came when we reached Akhura station near Agartala and where Wing Commander Daish's first question was, 'What happened at Parbatipur and where are the Medical Officer's cushions?' I had to make a formal report which highlighted the dreadful condition of the train and fortunately, as the cushions could be returned undamaged, the matter ended.

So after some tedious months spent in reforming, No. 27 (Beaufighter) Squadron found a permanent home from where regular operations could be made.

Although it only had one runway Agartala was a busy air force base. It comprised No. 169 Headquarters Wing, first under Wing Commander Elsdon, DFC, and later under Group Captain Champion de Crespigny, and three RAF squadrons: No. 5 Squadron with Curtiss Mohawk single-engine fighters which were subsequently replaced by No. 17 Squadron with Hurricanes under an Australian, Squadron Leader 'Bush' Cotton, DFC; No. 31 Squadron flying Douglas Dakota twin-engine supply-dropping transports under Wing Commander Burberry, DFC, AFC; and No. 27 Squadron, operating Beaufighter twin-engine long-range low-level attack fighters under Wing Commander H. C. Daish. In all, there were some fifty operational aircraft on the station. The army provided an anti-aircraft unit against Japanese air attacks and the RAF Regiment several hundred soldiers for aerodrome security.

The several thousand air force, army and unskilled Indian labourers who made up Agartala were billeted in their own squadrons and units, dispersed around the aerodrome. No. 27's living and mess quarters were about three miles from the aerodrome, known as No. 1 Camp, whilst the operations of the squadron were centrally located close to the aerodrome in a number of bamboo basha buildings comprising Headquarters, Stores, Maintenance, Armoury and the two Flights – 'A' and 'B'. As with the living quarters, the aircraft were dispersed over a wide area, some aircraft having a pen which comprised three ten-foot high earth walls for protection against bombing attacks. Otherwise, they stood on open stands cut out of the jungle, and, whenever possible, the front section of each aircraft was covered with a camouflage net. Daily maintenance and servicing of the aircraft was carried out by the seemingly tireless groundcrews at these locations; however, there were a couple of bamboo half hangars which were used for aircraft undergoing longer duration servicing, such as the forty-hour inspection.

Part of No. 169 Headquarters' responsibility was to provide the infrastructure to keep the three squadrons operationally effective. Matters such as aerodrome maintenance, building construction and maintenance, road construction and maintenance were their main responsibilities. There were no services such as electricity, water or sewerage as we were used to in our home countries and as our counterparts in Britain were enjoying. Most lighting was by kerosene or Tilly lamps. All drinking water was obtained from the mess kitchen where it was boiled before being released. For showering, the common procedure was for your bearer to heat a kerosene tin of water over an open fire which, when ready, was tipped into another kerosene tin with a perforated bottom, lifted onto a prearranged hook in a wash room which allowed you three or four minutes to soap up and shower off. We went through this exercise twice a day. The toilet amenity was, in my opinion, a work of art. Each toilet was a neat fifteen-inch wide hole in the ground that went down ten to twenty feet and it was interesting to watch the 'unskilled' Indian labourers digging these holes. They did it with two pieces of bamboo; one piece had a sharpened point and was used like a crowbar, the other was thicker and splayed at one end, which acted like a grab bucket. First, the sharp-pointed bamboo was used to break up the ground, then the split-ended bamboo was lowered into the hole and pressure applied to cause the splay end to open out. The pressure was then released, resulting in soil being held in the splayed bamboo, which was then raised from the hole.

The squadron accommodation was divided into three groups – officers, NCOs and airmen. All buildings were made of local materials – bamboo for the frames and walls, rush-type grass for the roof and handmade bricks for the floor. The bed was the traditional Indian charpoy to which we added our own camp bedding and mosquito net. Some degree of 'air conditioning' was provided by ceiling punkas in each basha hut that were activated by a punka wallah pulling on a rope at the end of each basha. This had the effect of moving the punka which, in turn, moved the air in the basha but, understandably, caused the punka wallah to doze off during hot afternoons when we were resting – naturally there would be a shout from one of us and for the next few minutes the punka would be most effective.

Having your own bearer, or sharing one, was optional. The occasional bearer was a professional, but generally they came from local villages and had very little contact with Europeans – before they could be employed they had to be security checked by No. 169 Wing. The years 1942 and 1943 were bad crop years, and standard payment was a gratefully received thirty pounds of rice per month drawn from the squadron rations and supplemented by personal handouts of clothing, food and cash. My bearer, Ali, whom I shared with Paddy, was a pleasant, quiet lad of about twenty. His day was from 6 am to 6 pm, during which time he organised an early cup of tea, fixed the morning and evening showers, organised laundry and generally kept our rooms clean and tidy. For the rest of the day the bearers were on standby and usually congregated at the rear of the huts from where they provided a security watch over their sahib's possessions and, no doubt, discussed who we were and what we were doing.

After Ali settled in, I asked him to obtain a rhesus monkey for me as a pet and so Modu – which means honey – joined the author's entourage. Modu quickly settled in and provided an extra guard for my property. She had a distinct dislike of Indians, which probably went back to mistreatment by her previous owner, and poor Ali suffered as a result. Whilst we got on as a threesome, it was a different story when I was not there and Ali had to make sure he kept out of her range – when he did not, she would inevitably sink her teeth into him and when this happened I had the job of restoring the peace. This was done by giving Ali some sweets to give to her. Modu was tied to a long

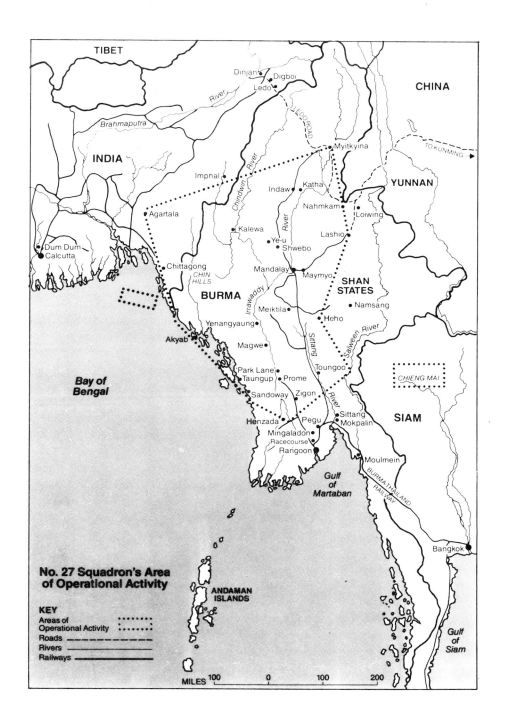

TIBET

CHINA

River

Brahmaputra

INDIA

Dinjan • • Digboi
Ledo •

LEDO ROAD

Myitkyina •

TO KUNMING →

Imphal •

Indaw • • Katha

YUNNAN

Chindwin River

Nahmkam •

• Loiwing

Agartala •

Kalewa •

Lashio •

Ye-u •
Shwebo •

Dum Dum
Calcutta •

River

Chittagong •

CHIN
HILLS

Mandalay • • Maymyo

Meiktila •

• Namsang

BURMA

Irrawaddy

SHAN
STATES

Heho •

Yenangyaung •

Salween River

Akyab •

Magwe •

Sittang

Toungoo •

Bay of
Bengal

CHIENG MAI

Park Lane •
Taungup • • Prome

Sandoway •

Zigon •

River

Henzada •

Pegu •

Sittang •
Mokpalin

SIAM

Mingaladon •
Racecourse •
Rangoon •

Moulmein •

BURMA-THAILAND RAILWAY

Gulf
of
Martaban

Bangkok •

**No. 27 Squadron's Area
of Operational Activity**

ANDAMAN
ISLANDS

KEY

Areas of Operational Activity	· · · · · · ·
Roads	– – – – – –
Rivers	————
Railways	▬▬▬▬

Gulf
of
Siam

MILES 100   0   100   200

lead that gave her a great deal of freedom outside my room but stopped short of letting her into the room which was her constant ambition, as personal articles which she could see in the room always attracted her attention. Once she slipped the lead, grabbed a bottle of aspirins, and shot up onto the roof where she consumed most of the aspirins. She quickly passed out and it was a few days before she was back to normal.

She was constantly on watch for me crossing the compound back to my room as she quickly learnt that it often resulted in something to eat, usually a banana. When the occasional parcel turned up from home it was a red letter day for Modu who invariably became part of the opening ceremony. The parcels were usually calico wrapped and securely sewn and Modu would become increasingly frustrated and annoyed as she tried to tear open the parcel.

The officers mess comprised a lounge-cum-dining area, a bar and a kitchen, all of which was in charge of the efficient Corporal Weir. Food rations were the same for officers, NCOs and airmen. Plenty of tinned bully beef, sausages and fish, and occasionally fresh local poultry and eggs. Once a week a truck was sent sixty miles to Comilla to pick up freshly-killed water buffalo which was immediately cooked to become pretty tough curry and rice. Tinned vegetables and fruit were supplemented by locally-grown fruits, such as bananas, pineapples and to a lesser extent, lychees. One pilot noted in his diary 'pineapples are now yellow, ripe and juicy, delighting the inner man'. Bread was baked each day. With limited generator power, there was little refrigeration and this was reserved for perishables such as butter.

Corporal Weir had a mess staff of BOR's and local helpers, supplemented by the officers' own bearers who acted as waiters for their sahibs. Some of the bearers were regulars; they were usually older men and obviously had come from other RAF or Army units. They dressed in mess kit and showed an expression of superiority over their fellow local wartime counterparts whose dress was the village dhoti.

Liquor rations were the same for officers and NCOs, comprising two bottles of local Murree or Australian 'Tiger' beer per man per month, local Carews or Hayward gin and rum. The officers usually gave their beer ration to the airmen whose ration was beer only, supplementing their own gin and rum ration with local purchases or whatever spirits that were available – and that was precious little initially, although later in the year things did improve.

Unless flying early, the aircrew went down to the 'drome each day at 8 am and returned at 12.30 pm. Going back to the 'drome in the afternoon was dependent on what special duties you were assigned, such as briefing for an operation the next day, air-testing an aircraft, compass swinging, harmonizing cannons/guns, Duty Officer, committee of adjustment, censoring of outgoing mail, etc. Without a special assignment, most aircrew spent the early afternoon in their rooms out of the heat.

Some aircrew were given specific duties, apart from flying, including: Flying Officer Franklin, Navigation and Lectures; Pilot Officer Clark, Mess; Pilot Officer House,

Intelligence; Pilot Officer Innes, Photography (using No. 169 Wing facilities); Pilot Officer Sterling, Parachute; Pilot Officer White, Fire (Headquarters); Pilot Officer Cross, Security (Headquarters); Pilot Officer Wandless, Fire and Security (No. 1 Camp); Pilot Officer Cotter, Sport; and Sergeant Spratt, Motor Transport.

The aerodrome had only one runway – it was an all weather concrete strip of 5500 by 150 feet running approximately north-east and south-west. The western half was flat but the eastern half had a nasty dip about 1000 feet from the end, which made landing from the 'roller coaster' eastern end more hazardous than landing from the west. A peculiarity of the aerodrome was a road that crossed the runway at right-angles and was open to approved public transport that had business with the camp. The road had boom gates on either side of the runway like a railway crossing – of course, aircraft movements had priority. There was an understanding with No. 31 Squadron, the supply-dropping Dakotas, that when Beaufighters were taking off, they would have priority. This was to help overcome the Beaufighters' sleeve-valve heating problem – something that did not worry the Dakotas which were constantly taking off and landing on supply dropping missions.

Around the aerodrome were anti-aircraft batteries and plenty of slit trenches – both came into use when Japanese aircraft made attacks. One of our exercises was to assist the anti-aircraft boys to calibrate their guns by flying straight and level at 10,000 feet with the ack-ack gun fuses set to explode at 6,000 feet. We did not regard it as a particularly healthy exercise, but one that was made a little more comfortable for the aircrews because we always carried one of their men.

So this was the general scene at Agartala when No. 27 Squadron finally settled down to carrying out regular operations. In summary, we were in the jungle a couple of hundred miles to the east of Calcutta. There were not too many home comforts like a local pub or cinema, bright lights or the fairer sex. There was certainly little to distract three Australian, two Canadian, one New Zealander, and thirty British aircrew from getting on with the job of harassing the Japanese, unless it was local politics, for on 20 February the officers were instructed to wear their revolvers at all times, as a precaution against the 'Free India Movement'.

5·PRE MONSOON ACTIVITIES – FEB./MAY, 1943

When we finally became operational in February 1943, we were notified that, contrary to the general scaling down of military operations that would take place during the monsoon period from May to October, we would be carrying out regular missions into Burma against the Japanese lines of communication right through the monsoon period.

The pattern of our missions was tied to the separate activities of the Allied armies and the Japanese plans to push into India. The Allied strategy to re-occupy Burma was confused to say the least. Subsequent records have confirmed that the British and the Americans did not see eye to eye on how Burma should be re-occupied.

The Americans placed great importance upon building-up China as a major base for offensives against the Japanese and the key to this was the need for a ground supply route from Assam, India, across northern Burma to China that would reduce the dependency on air transport over the Hump. By contrast, the British favoured a series of major Allied amphibious offensives against the Japanese in southern Burma, Malaya and the Dutch East Indies (now Indonesia).

For their part, the Japanese had reached the north-west Burma frontier with India by May 1942, and when the 1942 monsoon ended in October had built up a considerable force for an advance into India. At this time there was an increasing ground swell of civil unrest for independence in India and some front line troops were withdrawn to control the spreading riots and bombings. This was the era of the 'Free India Movement'. led by Subhas Chandra Bose who, naturally, had the support of the Japanese. In fact, the Japanese Army in Burma included some 5,000 Indian soldiers who had been recruited from those captured in Malaya. Bose referred to them as the Indian National Army and, although they did not engage in heavy civil fighting, their very presence was a nuisance factor that had to be watched.

In the Arakan, the end of 1942 found the Japanese strongly entrenched. Their 55th Division was able to prevent the 14th Indian Division from embarking on an amphibious attack on the port of Akyab. At this stage General Slim was sent to the Arakan to assess the situation and quickly realised the wisest course of action was to withdraw up the Arakan coast to Chittagong, leaving behind 2500 dead and the

Japanese in complete control of the Arakan. This was a humiliating defeat for the British and one which the Prime Minister, Churchill, found hard to understand.

With the 1943 monsoon only three months away there was no time to mount a major offensive against the Japanese in either the Arakan or northern Burma. This did not please General Chiang-Kai-shek and he would not commit Chinese troops to assist General Stilwell who was pushing ahead with a ground supply route from Ledo in Assam to the Japanese-occupied town of Mogaung, thirty miles south of Myitkyina. It was called the Ledo Road.

With this rather dismal background of military events, Field Marshal Wavell, Commander-in-Chief at New Delhi, decided the time had arrived to test, as a guerilla activity, Brigadier Orde Wingate's 'long range penetration' philosophy. Strategically, it could be very important for General Stilwell as the Japanese had decided the Ledo Road plans had gone far enough. Strong Japanese forces were sent along the Hukawng Valley to Shinbwiyang and the railway from Mandalay to Myitkyina which played a key role in their movements and would be a prime target for Wingate's Phantom Army, as it became known. So, on 7 February 1943, at Imphal, Assam, Field Marshal Wavell bid farewell to Wingate and his men.

Wingate was a remarkable soldier. Over twenty years his exploits in the Sudan, Palestine and Abyssinia were almost legendary. He became Commander-in-Chief to Emperor Haile Selassie of Abyssinia, earning the unofficial title of Lawrence of Abyssinia because of certain similarities to his distant but illustrious relative, Lawrence of Arabia. From these campaigns he returned to London in November 1941.

In March 1942, he was sent to join the staff of General Sir Archibald Wavell in Java, but the war was moving so swiftly that he found General Wavell's headquarters were back in New Delhi and it was from here that Wavell sent him to Burma to serve with General Alexander who had just taken over command of the British Army in Burma, with headquarters at Maymyo, east of Mandalay.

Wingate lectured the general staff on his theories of long range penetration, based on comparable experiences he had gained in Palestine and Abyssinia. Finally, in June 1942, with Burma completely in the hands of the Japanese, Wavell authorised Wingate to form a brigade on the lines he proposed. Wingate was able to obtain the services of senior officers who had worked with him or knew of his exploits. Thus he was able to appoint Majors Ferguson, Calvert and Bromhead as his key officers. The men of the brigade were a mixture of British troops, Gurkhas, commandos from the Bush Warfare School at Maymyo, Burma riflemen, Signallers, a mule transport company and some RAF officers who had volunteered for 'special duty'.

Wingate's philosophy was 'we've superior brains, resources, technique, spiritual background, outlook. Let's organise these things, use them intelligently, employ the weapons we have, and we'll beat the Jap.' So, for six months in India's Central Provinces, this brigade went through a jungle training experience like nothing that had ever previously been attempted. The three qualities listed by Wingate as essential for the specialised warfare for which the brigade was preparing were training, physical toughness and courage. By the end of 1942, those who survived had reached a point of preparation where they could be committed for the task of a Long Range Penetration Brigade that could operate within Japanese lines in Burma with everything they needed to survive dropped to them from the air.

When the Phantom Army left Imphal on 7 February 1943, it consisted of 3,000 men and 1,000 animals, including horses, oxen, mules and elephants. Its task was to travel 150 miles across enemy held territory, including the crossing of a major river, the Chindwin, well used roads and finally to straddle the main railway line which ran from Mandalay to Myitkyina and put it out of action. As the brigade approached the Chindwin River it split into two groups. No. 1 Group was the main diversionary group and after crossing the Chindwin River it took a south-east course. No. 2 Group was the main group and, after breaking away from No. 1 Group, it concealed its movements by travelling only at night. It turned north-east and finally crossed the Chindwin River some forty miles to the north of No. 1 Group. Its prime objective when it was within striking distance of the railway was for the colums of Majors Ferguson and Calvert to dash ahead and carry out demolition of the track, leaving the rest of No. 2 Group to carry out further diversionary attacks on the Japanese.

On 6 March, Major Ferguson's column successfully blew the two spans of the Bonchaung Bridge over which the railway crossed. The same evening, Major Calvert's column blasted a 200-yard section of high rocky cliffs from both sides of the Bonchaung Gorge. These operations effectively blocked the railway north of Bonchaung for many months to come. Continuing eastwards, all columns had crossed the Irrawaddy River by mid-March. It was never disclosed what the purpose was to be, but it seemed that if all had gone well Wingate would have attempted a surprise attack on the Japanese headquarters at Maymyo. In fact, forward units reached within forty miles of Lashio and sixty miles of Maymyo.

India Headquarters were now becoming concerned for the safety of the brigade and warned Wingate that if he advanced much further eastwards he would be out of range of supply dropping aircraft. They suggested an alternative operation on the Irrawaddy, but by now the Japanese had become fully aware of the brigade's activity and had brought up reinforcements from Mandalay in the south and from Fort Hertz and Yunnan in the north. Finally, on 24 March, India Headquarters ordered immediate withdrawal to India, and, on 27 March, the march back started. By now the brigade had been in enemy territory for seven weeks and was not in the same condition as when it had set out from Imphal on 7 February.

The brigade broke up into five groups and in turn into dispersal parties – each group independently determining its own route back to India. The first group back was Major Calvert's on 15 April, followed by Major Ferguson's on 25 April, then Brigadier

Wingate's on 29 April, and the fourth, Major Scott's, on 1 June. The fifth group, led by Major Gilkes, had opted to head east to China, rather than west to India. Eventually, they met local guerillas who provided guides, and, on 30 May, they reached Paoshan on the Burma Road. On 7 June, whilst being driven in motor lorries by the Chinese Army to Kunming, they were stopped by an American army officer, Major Clarke, a transport officer, who, upon hearing their story, took over their transportation back to India. There was an airfield nearby and he quickly called up all aircraft flying the 'Hump' that day – by then one Dakota or Commando aircraft was taking off every three minutes – and within a matter of hours the final group was back in India.

Subsequently, Brigadier Wingate paid special tribute to the RAF, especially to the transport aircraft which made many sorties to drop their life blood needs.

Unfortunately, there was no back-up ground force available that could have moved further into Burma, and so capitalise on the efforts of Wingate's men. What did happen was that the Japanese were thrown into a state of confusion from February to June 1943; some 10 – 15,000 of their troops became involved in countering Wingate's campaign, which helped the Chinese in the Salween River area, and some planned Japanese operations were called off, including against the Kachin Levies and against Stilwell's Ledo Road project.

Although No. 27 Squadron's early operations in northern Burma were linked to what Wingate was doing in Burma, No. 31 Squadron, also stationed at Agartala, was more closely associated with the Wingate campaign. In all, No. 31 Squadron made 175 supply dropping missions which provided Wingate with 300 tons of stores and equipment, without which the campaign would not have been possible.

Fortunately, the Wingate experience of 1943 was taken into full account when the Allied offensive in northern Burma was launched in March 1944. Instead of men marching 150 miles across enemy-occupied territory as Wingate's men had done, 10,000 men were landed from gliders, towed by Dakotas. They straddled the railway line from Mandalay to Myitkyina at places they called 'Aberdeen', 'Broadway', and 'Chowringhee'. The purpose was to disrupt the Japanese opposing Stilwell's southward drive from Ledo. It was a tragedy that Wingate, who was playing a leading role in the campaign, was killed on 24 March when his aircraft, piloted by an American crew, crashed on a Naga mountain whilst flying through a storm.

From 9 February, No. 27 Squadron's flying operations took on a regular pattern, with a sortie every two or three days. Originally, the tendency was for sorties to comprise four or six aircraft, but it did not take long to determine that where an operation involved a stretch of rail, road or river, two aircraft were more effective. However, when it was an attack on an aerodrome or a troop concentration four or six aircraft were used, whereby greater impact in a short period of time, in a concentrated area could be achieved. Disregarding the two operations that had been made at Christmas, the squadron was now fulfilling its role of harassing the Japanese lines of communication in Burma, and this meant many of the aircrews were flying on operations for the first time and into territory where there was little background information upon what to expect. Whenever possible, the pattern for a two-aircraft operation was one experienced and one inexperienced crew.

There remained about two and a half months before the monsoon really set in, and during this period twenty-five operations were made, involving eighty-two Beaufighters. The operations were widely spread over Burma – six in the north, eleven in central, three in southern, and five in the Arakan. The targets comprised aerodromes at Shwebo, Magwe, Park Lane, Toungoo, Tennant, Kalaywe, Kyungun, He-Ho and Prome. Other targets were rail, road and river transport and installations, as well as warehouses and troop concentrations. In February, as a result of enemy action, two aircraft and their crews were lost. The first, crewed by Pilot Officers Townsend and Wandless, was brought down by ground fire whilst attacking He-Ho aerodrome, and the second, flown by Squadron Leader Illingworth, DFC, and Sergeant Osguthorpe, was lost whilst attacking Prome aerodrome. In the latter case, Pilot Officer Thompson with Pilot Officer Merritt, who were flying close by along the Irrawaddy River, saw the actual hits to Illingworth's aircraft, which they estimated to be 40 mm Bofors cannon. After being hit, the aircraft rolled slowly onto its back before crashing to the ground. This was not a very good start, and it certainly made us aware that the Japanese had strong aerodrome defences.

On another operation, Sergeant Hartness finished an attack on Toungoo aerodrome so low that he hit a tall teak stump which smashed the leading edge of his starboard wing between the engine and fuselage, as well as denting the front cowling of the engine. That he was able to fly his aircraft back to Agartala was a testimony to the strength of the Beau, but a little dicey.

March started off with the squadron being placed on standby for the first few days by No. 224 Group, but to our disappointment we did not carry out a single operation.

The standby was linked to Wingate's Phantom Army, whose No. 2 Group was approaching its prime target – the railway line in the Bonchaung Gorge area. Our standby targets were to be rolling stock and all enemy movements on the railway line between Shwebo and Indaw, excluding the town of Kyngon. At the same time, RAF bombers were bombing the towns of Katha, Naba and Wuntho, where the Japanese had camps and, as already mentioned, the successful blowing of the Bonchaung railway bridge and the walls of the gorge by Wingate's men took place on the night of 6 March.

The operations which the squadron carried out during March were in the Arakan and Central Burma. In the Arakan, the operations, organised by Group, involved other RAF squadrons and different aircraft – Hurricanes and Blenheims – and the targets were shipping and aerodromes on the islands of Akyab and Ramree. The Hurricanes were to provide top cover, the Blenheims were to unload their bombs and the

Beaufighters were to carry out low-level strafing. Twice this exercise – involving ten Beaufighters – was carried out, but a combination of the Beaufighter's faster speed at low level and bad weather resulted in both operations not running to plan. In fact, it proved a costly exercise for No. 27 Squadron. One aircraft and its crew, Flight Lieutenant McMichael and Sergeant Dodd, were lost, and two other aircraft were damaged – all as a result of accurate ground fire. One of the damaged aircraft was the CO's, who was leading six Beaufighters in attacks on ground installations. He had successfully blown up an oil dump. However, he did not know that a bullet had passed through the undercarriage, bursting a tyre, and resulting, during a night landing at Agartala, in the aircraft swinging off the runway, causing the port undercarriage to collapse.

This accident was a lesson for all of the pilots as you never knew until your wheels firmly touched the runway on return from operations that the same thing might have happened to you. Therefore, when landing after an operation, the pilots, apart from visually checking their tyres from the cockpit for possible damage, adopted a degree of expectancy that their tyres may have been hit and were thus extra alert to respond to the effect that a burst tyre would have on the performance of their aircraft once it had touched down on the runway.

It turned out that Flight Lieutenant McMichael and Sergeant Dodd were taken prisoners by the Japanese and survived the ordeal, and were released in 1945.

On two successive days, 18 and 19 March, and again on the 26, fifteen Beaufighters were used to attack aerodromes in Central Burma at Toungoo, Tennant, Kalaywa and Kyungon, as well as railways and roads in the area. At least three Japanese aeroplanes were destroyed on the ground, one T45 fighter-bomber by the author and two Army 0.1 S/S fighters. Considerable rolling stock, road transport and buildings, including army barracks, were shot up. Most of the Beaufighters were hit by ground fire. In one instance three aircraft piloted by Squadron Leader Statham, AFC, Sergeant Johnson and the author were chased by three Japanese fighters after attacking Toungoo aerodrome. Our speed enabled us to keep out of the range of their guns and when we could no longer see them we throttled back to cruising speed. However, they had apparently decided to keep on our track and when my navigator, Paddy, called me over the intercom to say they were in sight again and closing on us, I opened the throttles to full power. Simultaneously, I called Statham and Johnson to warn them and to advise I was increasing speed, but Statham never replied. Yet, he must have seen Johnson and me move ahead as we were in close formation. Very quickly the Japanese fighters had his aircraft within range and shot him down. In such happenings one can only guess what might have happened – either he, or his navigator, or the aircraft, had been hit when we were attacking Toungoo and he was unable to respond to the warning I had given or to the action Sergeant Johnson and I had taken.

Another operation involved an attack by three Beaufighters on Prome Town and transit camp, five minutes after Blenheims from Nos 16 and 113 Squadrons had bombed the camp. This was a very good exercise and much damage was done by the respective aircraft. Prome was to become a prime target for it was a key Japanese centre for the supply of men and equipment to the Arakan. It was to feature in many attacks in the months to come.

During February and March, seven aircrews of No. 177 Squadron had joined us at Agartala. This new Beaufighter squadron was to be based at nearby Pharpamau and pending the aerodrome being prepared for Beaufighters and the groundstaff being established, these aircrews were given the opportunity to participate with their No. 27 counterparts and learn what to expect when their squadron began operations. Some flew with us as passengers whilst others flew as operational crews, and sadly this was not a very successful experience. Within a very short time they had lost three of their seven crews, including that of the Commanding Officer elect, Squadron Leader Statham, AFC, and Pilot Officer Briffett. The other crews were Squadron Leader Illingworth, DFC, and Sergeant Osguthorpe; Flight Lieutenant McMichael and Sergeant Dodd, the latter crew as already mentioned surviving the war as prisoners of war.

The squadron received visits during March from the AOC AHQ Bengal, Air Vice Marshal Williams; the AOC No. 224 Group, Air Commodore Gray, MC; five senior Group Officers involved with Intelligence, Armament, Photography and Training; plus a representative of the Bristol Aircraft Company, Mr J. Woodhouse, as well as the Lady Mary Herbert, wife of H. E., the Governor of Bengal.

It seemed that '27' had become of age and this became more apparent when, early in April, General (later Field Marshal) Auchinleck, who was about to take over from Field Marshal Wavell, paid a visit, whilst on 1 April the entire squadron was paraded and inspected by the Maharajah of Tripura to celebrate the tenth anniversary of the Indian Air Force.

Throughout April no sorties were flown in Northern Burma. No doubt this was because Wingate's men were making their way back to India. Although they had their supplies dropped from the air by No. 31 Squadron, they did not need air support of the type that we could provide.

For the first time, operations were carried out by No. 27's Beaufighters in Southern Burma – that is, in the country below Prome, to just north of Rangoon. For some of the sorties flown to Central and Eastern Burma, such as Toungoo and He-Ho aerodromes, we refuelled at forward aerodromes close to the India/Burma border in the Arakan – Ramu, Reindeer or Dohazari were the usual places. Sometimes, it meant an overnight stop and an early morning take-off. These forward refuelling aerodromes became quite significant as they allowed us to fly further into Burma, as well as providing refuelling points on the return flights from long sorties north of Rangoon or down the Arakan coast to Cape Negrais, west of Rangoon.

Apart from an attack on the aerodrome at Magwe, where one fighter on the ground was damaged, and on the aerodromes at Park Lane and Taungup, most sorties were along the Irrawaddy River and the Arakan coast, resulting in considerable damage to all forms of river craft. Double-deck steamers, barges and hundreds of sampans felt the sting of the Beaufighters' cannons and machine guns. Damage was also inflicted on rolling stock on the railway between Prome and Henzada, including engines, wagons, stations and signal boxes. Rolling stock and river craft in the Mandalay/Monywa area were targets at the end of the month and again considerable damage was done to both rail and river transport.

Our losses in April were one aircraft and the crew of Sergeants Ensor and Clough, who flew into the sea off the Arakan coast. This was particularly unfortunate – or more correctly, careless – as the CO had warned the crews in the preflight briefing that they must not fly below the level of his aircraft when over the sea as, in the absence of wind, they would be flying over a glassy sea where the chances of unintentionally flying lower and lower was always a possibility.

The Japanese must have decided it was time to retaliate against us and on 6 April at least eighteen Army 97 bombers escorted by a dozen or so fighters attacked Agartala. The damage could have been worse; the runway was hit but was serviceable within one hour, one Beaufighter and one USAAF Lockheed Lightning, which had landed to refuel, were hit by shrapnel. Two squadron bowsers, the 'A' flight office and the watchtower were burnt out. We lost a motorcycle, a tractor, some stores and ammunition. Two of the squadron's personnel were injured out of a total of six on the station, whilst twenty-five Indian civilians were killed and fourteen injured. The Japanese had used high explosive and anti-personnel bombs as well as a large number of phosphorous and rubber incendiary bombs. Paddy's diary recorded the occasion in the following words:

Black day! Told off by the CO. Bombed by Japs. See horrible sights. Feel sick and am bloody brassed off. Feel like resigning, getting out of this bloody country.

What had upset Paddy was that I had used my bush shirt to apply a tourniquet to one of the squadron's injured airmen and when conditions returned to normal we went to the mess for a cup of tea. I was in a singlet and this is what caused the CO to remind me I should be properly dressed at all times in the mess. Paddy's diary for the next day read:

Feeling better. Blokes don't half scatter when the warning goes.

So much for the Irish!

One week later the presence of Beaufighters in India was released to the general public through the Indian newspapers. In the course of the official Public Relations release, interviews were made with some of the squadron personnel about operations and so on. The classic interview was with the CO's navigator, Frankie, who when asked what he did prior to the war, said, 'I used to put on my little bowler hat and catch the train to the city where I was in the Foreign Exchange Market.'

Three more Beaufighter crews posted to No. 177 Squadron joined us for operational experience. However, on 26 April all of the attached crews proceeded to Pharpamau to form the first flight of that squadron and it soon became evident that before long they would be operational.

6 · THE MONSOON –
MAY-OCTOBER 1943

Modern jets flying across Burma and the Bay of Bengal today at 35,000 feet are able to avoid the monsoonal weather that had to be faced by the Allied forces, both army and air force, in 1942, 1943, 1944 and 1945. Each theatre of war had its special features, and although we did not have to face the flak of Europe, the five or six months of monsoon conditions were not fun to those who flew in them, whilst on the ground we all had to live with prickly heat, dhobi itch, dysentry, heatstroke, malaria and, above all, boredom.

The month before the 1942 monsoon was the hottest in Calcutta for eighty years, with considerable numbers of Indians dying in the streets, their bodies remaining uncollected. At Allahabad, Central India, where No. 22 Ferry Control was stationed, 200 out of 700 airmen were stricken by heat exhaustion and seven died. I spent some time there after an operational tour on No. 27 Squadron, and it was not much different with most days 120 degrees Fahrenheit in the shade. All work, including flying, ceased at 10 am following a dawn start. On one occasion, a single-engine aeroplane ahead of me was given the green light to take off but did not move – the pilot had passed out with the heat. All we could do from 10 am was stay in our room where a local innovation, the Khus-Khus, gave some relief. It was a screen made from an interwoven native shrub that fitted the open door of your room, where one bearer kept it wet with water, thus cooling the hot Sind desert air that entered our room, whilst a second bearer operated the overhead room punka. These Khus-Khus wallahs and punka wallahs, as they were known, must surely have saved some airmen's lives.

In May each year, after two months of damp, stifling, hot, oppressive weather, a wind, gentle at first, enters the Bay of Bengal from the equator and soon it has enough power to raise moisture from the sea. The Himalayas then deflect its direction east and west, resulting in storms breaking out in Bengal and the Indian frontier with Burma. Conditions on the ground suddenly become even more unpleasant – especially for new arrivals – and, it is said, make flying there the most perilous in the world. To give credence to this, five Hurricanes returning from a sortie over the Chin Hills, with fuel running short, had no option but to fly into cumulonimbus clouds. Two made it back to base, the other three were never found. On another occasion the sixteen Spitfires of No. 615 Squadron, when flying from Palel back to Calcutta, unwisely flew into cumulo-nimbus clouds, resulting in the loss of eight aircraft and four pilots, including the Commanding Officer, Squadron Leader McCormack, DFC, an Australian. As another illustration, Dakota supply dropping transports were known to take six or seven days eventually to make one successful drop to a prearranged DZ (dropping zone). There was not a pilot in No. 27 Squadron who did not abort at least one sortie during the monsoon period.

The monsoon begins in May and blows itself out in October. Viewed from the ground, a typical storm first appears in the distance as a grey-blue cloud mass, turning grey-black and by the time it strikes, the wind is of gale force and accompanied by torrential rain and lightning. Just north of Agartala is one of the world's heaviest rainfall areas, about 500 inches annually, whilst in the Arakan 200 inches falls in five months.

At the beginning of the 1943 monsoon in May, the Japanese withdrew most of their air force from Burma, in conformity with what the Allied and Japanese armies did, thus resulting in a general winding down of ground fighting. Most of the Japanese aircraft went back to Siam, many of them to Chengmai, in the mountains of northern Siam. In recent years I have visited Chengmai on three occasions and found that it would have been paradise to be stationed there in 1943 compared to our conditions in east Bengal during the monsoon.

In the air there was only one wise course of action under monsoon conditions – stay away from storms and avoid flying into cumulo-nimbus clouds, and we learnt to do this from practical experience. Flying in to Burma meant twice crossing the Lushai Hills, or the Naga Hills, or the Arakan Yomas, some of which exceeded 9,000 feet, and electrical storms were very much a part of the so-called hills and yomas. At all times we flew close to the mountain tops to minimise the chance of being seen or of being picked up on Japanese warning systems. Ideally, we always kept the mountain tops in visual sight, but flying became difficult when the cloud came down to the mountains, for then your navigator had his work cut out to find a way around the problem and still reach the target, or to determine finally that there was no reasonably safe way through, bearing in mind that in two or three hours, after completing the sortie, you had to get back to base. About that time, the middle of 1943, pathfinding over Europe was becoming a very valuable tool for RAF Bomber Command, and, in hindsight, it would be fair to say that most of our operations in the monsoon period were of a 'pathfinding' nature, requiring considerable skills by both navigators and pilots. The heat of the day caused massive cloud build-up and generally early morning sorties had a greater chance of being accomplished than afternoon sorties. It was always very comforting when after completing a sortie you started climbing the mountains on the Burma side to see sunlight away in the west towards India. What was an added problem with the early morning sorties was the local ground fogs which closed the aerodromes and a number of sorties had to be postponed for this reason, usually to the afternoon when the fog had lifted, but by then only time would tell if the operation could be accomplished because of the cloud build up over the mountains.

For the RAF squadrons who were to remain active in Burma throughout the monsoon of 1943 the operational strategy was:

to maintain a forward fighter offensive policy;

to ensure the continuance of local air superiority;

to protect coastal shipping south of Chittagong;

to attack enemy occupied airfields wherever possible;

to attack enemy lines of communication and shipping in the enemy forward areas.

From May to October 1943, No. 27 Squadron carried out 165 operations, involving 349 aircraft. The targets were widely spread over Burma – thirty-eight in the north, eighty-five in central, eight in southern, and thirty-four in the Arakan. Because of weather conditions during this six-month period, seventy-four aircraft had to abort their operations, thus reducing the number of completed sorties to 275. During the same period, No. 31 Squadron, based at Agartala, made 1,100 supply dropping sorties, using 'parajutes', an Indian substitute for the shortage of silk parachutes that had developed in Allied air forces by the sheer number of aeroplanes that were being put into commission. The duration of the Dakota flights was considerably less than those of the Beaufighters as their activities were linked to Allied ground forces operating along the India/Burma border.

Every Beaufighter crew could tell his own 'monsoon story'. One of the author's concerns a sortie to strafe Prome transit camp. In deteriorating weather and climbing over the Lushai Hills, I lost my No. 2 in cloud and was flying alone in rather bumpy conditions when all hell seemed to break loose. The aircraft was virtually out of my control until it broke cloud, heading at a great rate of knots for the mountain tops, and in the opposite direction to the one I had been flying when we entered cloud. The operation was then aborted and on returning to base I found that my No. 2 aircraft, crewed by Flying Officer White and Pilot Officer Cross, had already landed. It was their first operation and it made them wonder what they were in for over the next few months.

The targets during the monsoon period were primarily Japanese lines of communication – rail, road, river, sea – as well as troop concentrations and oil installations. The aerodromes in Burma received less attention for, as has already been mentioned, the Japanese had withdrawn most of their aircraft to Siam. They kept a few reconnaissance aircraft and some fighters in Burma to ensure that we did not have an open go. However, it was ground fire that was our main concern, and it resulted in many hits to the Beaufighers. The higher proportion of hits were towards the rear of our aircraft, indicating those firing on the ground were probably underestimating the speed of the Beaufighter and therefore were not allowing sufficient deflection. This was not much joy for our navigators who were situated towards the rear of the aircraft and were in fact hit more often than the pilots. On one occasion a bullet hit the water bottle behind Paddy's legs, spraying him and his cupola with water – he was not very happy.

Of the forty-three individual sorties made in May, ten were aborted because of bad weather, whilst another four did not take off from Agartala for the same reason. One of the successful operations during May was flown by Flight Lieutenant Swift and Pilot Officer Clark, and Sergeant Gunn and Flight Sergeant Noble. At Pyinmana, they came across one hundred Japanese soldiers on a parade ground and made four attacks, inflicting considerable casualties, as well as damaging huts within the camp.

As well as an attack on He-Ho aerodrome, where one aircraft was destroyed and another damaged on the ground, successful missions were carried out on the oil refinery at Yathaya, the Prome transit camp and rivercraft along the Irrawaddy River and the Kaladan River in the Arakan. Another attempt was made to carry out an operation with Hurricanes, this time into Burma, the idea being that two Beaufighters would act as navigator (pathfinder?) for an operation which the Hurricanes would not otherwise make. Two Hurricanes were fitted with long-range fuel tanks. Flight Sergeant Spratt and I joined them at Chittagong for a three-hour return flight to the Ye-u, Monywa area where we were to attack railway rolling stock and the aerodrome at Monywa. Climbing over the 9000-foot Lushai Hills presented an immediate problem, as the two Hurricanes, with extra fuel on board, could not keep up with the Beaufighters which we had literally 'hanging on their propellors' at 130 knots. They soon turned back, leaving the Beaufighters to complete the operation.

Much to the surprise of those at the aerodrome on the morning of 11 April, a strange aircraft approached and was quickly identified as a De Havilland Mosquito. Mosquito Mk II DZ695 was to be attached to us for weather trials and operational familiarisation, becoming the first Mosquito sent to the tropics for this purpose. The crew, Flight Lieutenants McCullock, DFC, and Young, had flown the aircraft from the UK. One week later, a second Mosquito, crewed by Flying Officer Fielding and Flight Sergeant Steer, and on 2 May a third, crewed by Flying Officers Dupee, DFM, and McDonnell, were attached for the same purpose. Their arrival was to coincide with the approaching monsoon season and, no doubt, had been deliberately chosen to expose the Mosquitos to the tropical elements. Simultaneously, a representative of the de Havilland Aircraft Company, Mr Myers, was attached to the squadron whilst Mr Waterhouse, a Rolls-Royce representative, made a short visit – no doubt both would be keeping an eye on the Mosquito's performance.

As the 1939-45 war progressed, the Mosquito was to become known as 'The Wooden Wonder', because of the extensive use of wood in its airframe construction. It was developed by the de Havilland Aircraft Company as an unarmed bomber which relied upon speed for defence and early in 1940 the RAF ordered fifty from the drawing boards; the first prototype flew in mid-1940. The Mosquito went on to become an

Wing Commander James B. Nicholson, VC, DFC, making a recording for the British Broadcasting Corporation in South-East Asia just before he was killed in May 1945.

Flight Lieutenant James B. Nicholson before the Battle of Britain, 1940, in which campaign he was awarded the Victoria Cross for destroying an enemy aircraft while his Hurricane was in flames, and he sustained serious burns.

Wing Commander (later Group Captain) Frank Carey, DFC, and Bars, DFM, was commanding officer of the Air Fighting Training Unit at Amarda Road in 1943.

Captain Pete Sanders, who was attached to No. 27 Squadron at Agartala in 1943 as Army liaison officer.

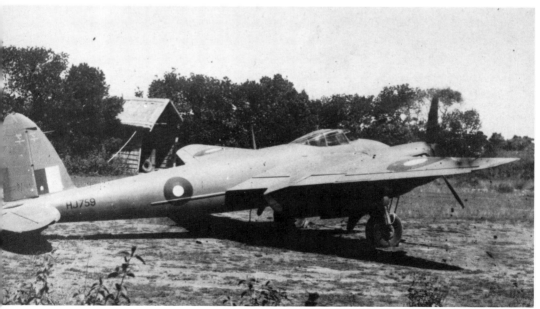

The first Mosquitos sent to the tropics for weather and operational trials were attached to No. 27 Squadron at Agartala in April 1943. They were Mark II. HJ759 was one of the first.

The No. 27 Squadron aircrew soccer team at Agartala in 1943.

'It ain't half hot mammie'. No. 27 Squadron's concert party, Agartala, 1943.

Opposite top and bottom, and above: typical servicing conditions at Agartala. The use of camouflage netting is of interest, the base being only some one hundred miles from Japanese-occupied Burma.

Beaufighter Mk VIF X8092, *R* of No. 27 Squadron, on trestles at the firing butts at Agartala for cannon and machine-gun alignment, in March 1943.

A Japanese oil dump in a railway siding after being shot up.

A Japanese oil barge on the Irrawady River burns after a Beaufighter attack.

Cannon strikes on an Irrawaddy River steamer.

Cannon strikes on Japanese tanks loaded on a military train at Kume Road in Central Burma.

Cannon attack on the railway marshalling yard at Pyinmana in 1943.

Rupert is growing up.

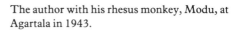
The author with his rhesus monkey, Modu, at Agartala in 1943.

Modu, the monkey, with Elsie and Rupert, the Himalayan bears, at Agartala in 1943.

The Raja of Tripura's Palace at Agartala, Ujjayanta Palace. Agartala is the State Capital of Tripura.

Darjeeling and Mount Kanchenjunga.

On leave at Srinagar, Kashmir, in 1943.

The author with a three-pound Kashmir trout, caught on leave.

One of 'Triggy' Trigwell's confirmed Beaufighters.

What a crashed Beaufighter looks like!

Squadron Leader George Bassingthwaight, DFC, generally known at B16, who became Flight Commander of 'B' Flight in January 1944, and his famous Australian bull, Woodlands Beaufighter, 1968.

Chota Bo Dekko — Little Bo Peep, a special fourteen-inch camera fitted to the author's Beaufighter.

Strikes on oil carrying Japanese road transport, left, and opposite what happened to the oil-carrying road transport.

Cannon attacks on a Japanese supply train south of Mandalay.

Shelters to protect Japanese trains from daylight Beaufighter attacks.

Squadron Leader Horn and Warrant Officer Blake being de-briefed by Flying Officer Wakelin, the squadron intelligence officer, with Wing Commander Daish looking on.

An after mission de-briefing by the squadron's intelligence officer.

Officers of No. 27 Squadron 'on rest' at Cholavaram, Madras, in 1944.

No. 27 Squadron aircrew being inspected by Lord Louis Mountbatten at Chiringer in 1945.

The author and Paddy Sterling and the RAF Museum's Beaufighter in 1983, and holding Nicholson's Victoria Cross.

extremely versatile aircraft, being used for low-level attacks using cannon, machine guns, rockets and bombs, high-level photo reconnaissance, pathfinding with Bomber Command, and torpedo dropping with the Royal Navy. It was the first British twin-engined aircraft to land on an aircraft carrier, HMS *Indefatigable.*

Compared to the Beaufighter, it was lighter on the controls, weighed about the same and was powered by two Rolls-Royce Merlin inline liquid-cooled engines, rather than air-cooled radials. At ground level its speed was, if anything, slightly faster than the Beaufighter and, in Burma when with No. 27 Squadron, the aircraft were armed with four 20 mm cannons (the same as the Beau) and four 0.303-in machine guns (the Beau carried six). With a range similar to the Beaufighter's, it comfortably fitted into the scale of operations we were carrying out with the Beaufighters. The first reaction of the Beaufighter crews at Agartala was one of reservation, for the Mosquito did not seem to have the airframe strength desirable for low-level attacks where there was always the risk of aircraft hitting objects such as trees during attacks.

The first Mosquito operation was made by Flying Officers Dupee, DFM, and McDonnell on 19 May, along the railway in central Burma where a moving train was attacked and stopped. The same crew carried out the second Mosquito operation on 29 May, this time a reconnaissance of aerodromes in the Kangaung, Meiktila, Thedaw and He-Ho area. Over He-Ho they encountered an Army 0.1 fighter and, like the Beaufighter, they were able to avoid an attack by the Japanese aeroplane by the sheer speed of the Mosquito at ground level – no doubt the Japanese would have liked the opportunity to attempt to shoot it down.

Losses during the month were one Beaufighter, crewed by Flying Officer Sturrock and Sergeant Heywood, and it is believed that they were hit by ground fire during an attack on a train in the Shanywa area. There were two accidents as a result of engine failures – the first, a Beaufighter crewed by Sergeant Graham and Warrant Officer Powdrill, when cannon testing in the sea at the mouth of the Ganges River. Sergeant Graham was able to carry out a forced landing on nearby Hatia Island, neither of the crew being injured. The second accident was to a Mosquito, crewed by Flying Officer Fielding and Flight Sergeant Steer, which overran the Agartala runway when making an emergency single-engine landing; both crew were injured, Steer sustaining a fractured spine.

By now, No. 27 Squadron's original base in India at Amarda Road had been turned into an Air Firing Training Unit (AFTU), primarily for single-engine fighters. However, it was decided to send a Beaufighter to two of the ten-day courses in gunnery and tactics; Flying Officer Williams with his navigator, Flying Officer Herbert, participated in the first course, whilst the author and his navigator, Pilot Officer Sterling, participated in the second. The Commanding Officer of the AFTU was Wing Commander Frank Carey, DFC and Bars, DFM, who had distinguished himself as a pilot, first in the Battle of Britain, then in the 1942 evacuation from Burma, and finally in the first Allied Arakan offensive late in 1942. Later, as a group captain, he became the 'backroom boy' of the Burma victory in air supremacy. We certainly gained some valuable air-to-air gunnery practice on drogues, and in making quarter attacks on Hurricanes using cine-guns, as well as carrying out exercises with the Beaufighter acting as the evading aircraft and the Hurricanes using cine-guns as the attacking aircraft.

Experienced instructors like Squadron Leader McCormack, DFC and Bar, and Squadron Leader Bassingthwaighte, DFC, both Australians, flew with us to learn of the Beaufighter's capabilities, not least the value of its heavy armament for air-to-ground targets, as well as its speed compared to the Hurricane at low level. It was generally agreed that the use of the two types of aircraft on the same mission was not very practical and that it would be better for the Beaufighters to operate independently of other types of aircraft.

The weather in the first ten days of June was very bad and only one operation, a low-level attack on the Kangaung aerodrome by two Mosquitos, reached the target. They damaged three aircraft on the ground, one of which was probably destroyed. Four Army 0.1 fighters were over the aerodrome at 3-4000 feet, but made no attempt to attack the Mosquitos. Both aircraft encountered weather problems on the way back. In addition, DZ696, piloted by Flying Officer Dupee, DFM, developed a glycol leak in the starboard engine and made a single-engine flight to Cox's Bazaar, where on landing one of the tyres burst. As a result of the two problems the aircraft became uncontrollable, causing the port undercarriage to collapse. Both of the crew escaped injury.

In all, there were forty-eight individual sorties in June, of which twenty-two had to be aborted because of weather, as well as a further four being postponed on three successive days because of the weather conditions at Agartala. June was the worst month for weather as these figures show – for the first time, oxygen was used by some crews returning from operations to allow them to get above cloud formations that were covering the mountain tops. This month saw a concentration of attacks on river and, to a lesseer degree, sea craft, Group Headquarters no doubt taking the view that in this kind of weather, the rivers and ocean would be the most logical way for the Japanese to move stores, equipment and possibly men to the fronts. Consequently steamers, barges and sampans, as well as warehouses and oil installations along the rivers, were the main targets.

One Beaufighter was lost on operations, crewed by Flight Sergeant Petch and Sergeant Thomas. They were last seen flying normally at 1000-1500 feet along the Arakan coast between Satthwa and Zigon. Another aircraft was destroyed as a result of a cross-wind landing at Chittagong where it was putting down to refuel for an operation into central Burma. Three other aircraft had lucky escapes. Sergeant Gunn hit a tree at Pyawbwe, causing extensive damage to the starboard wing, Flying Officer Hassell hit unseen trip wires at Gwa Bay, which damaged the port undercarriage door, the exhaust and the airscrew, whilst Sergeant Hartness 'collected' an iron rod that was protruding from the top of a pagoda, which wrapped itself around the port wing and effectively locked the aileron. All three aircraft were flown back to Agartala and the fact they had been rather badly damaged indicates how tough were the Beaufighters. One could only surmise what would have happened if the aircraft had been Mosquitos.

After just two months with us, the two surviving Mosquitos and the three crews were posted to No. 681 Squadron, a Spitfire photo-reconnaissance unit at Dum Dum, Calcutta, where they were to begin Photographic Reconnaissance trials.

With the intention of improving amenities, and at the same time providing some relief against boredom for all members of the squadron, a lecture room was opened during June, and its use will be referred to in the next chapter.

This month VIP visits included Wing Commander Ulyatt, Roman Catholic Padre in Chief, and Dr Hubback, Bishop of Assam, both of whom conducted services for all members of the Squadron.

The weather in July showed a turn for the better, and out of sixty-two individual sorties, only twelve were aborted, a significantly better strike rate than in June, when the comparable figures were forty-eight and twenty-two. Nearly half of the sorties in July were made to central Burma, with the remainder to Northern Burma and the Arakan.

Following the June target pattern, no attacks were made on aerodromes in July, and the main activity was a heavy concentration of attacks on rivercraft along the Irrawaddy – in fact, it was not until the middle of the month that other targets were attacked. These included railways in Northern Burma, the Arakan waterways and the Prome Taungup road, which by now was referred to as the 'milkrun'. All types of rivercraft and installations were attacked – paddle steamers, launches, barges and sampans – as well as rail and road transport and oil storage installations. In the Gwa Bay area on the Arakan coast, a wooden road bridge was badly damaged, whilst a radio communication station with a 100-foot mast was located and attacked by Squadron Leader Horn and Warrant Officer Blake on a bank of the Chindwin River, between Kadu and Kindat in the far north of Burma. No doubt it was a link between the Japanese forces along the Burma/India border and their headquarters back at Maymyo.

Casualty-wise, July was a good month, for no aircraft were lost. One aircraft, crewed by Pilot Officer Cotter and Flight Sergeant Cooper, was hit by small arms fire over Padaung, near Prome. Cotter suffered wounds to both shins and the aircraft suffered damage to the airspeed indicator and the undercarriage, which had to be pumped down by hand. He was able to land the aircraft safely at Agartala, where he was bandaged up and sent to Comilla Field Hospital.

In July, the Commanding Officer, Wing Commander Daish, was posted to Air Headquarters Bengal at Barrackpore as Wing Commander Organisation, and we were all sorry to hear the news. In this posting he was to become reunited with two old RAF friends with whom he had been associated in England – Air Vice Marshal Williams, the AOC Bengal Command, and Air Commodore Mason. Air Headquarters Bengal at Barrackpore subsequently moved forward to Comilla to become 3rd Tactical Air Force and about a year later returned to Calcutta as Headquarters, Bengal/Burma. Wing Commander Daish was with Air Headquarters throughout this period, becoming Group Captain, Organisation.

It was not long before we heard that our new Commanding Officer was to be Wing Commander Nicolson, VC, a Battle of Britain fighter pilot. At the end of July, Squadron Leader Birt arrived from No. 42 (Hurricane) Squadron and assumed command of 'B' Flight from Flight Lieutenant Swift, who, in August, was posted to Combined War Room Operations, Colombo, Ceylon. With the departure of Daish and Swift, the author was the only Australian remaining of the original aircrew posted to No. 27 Squadron. However, two other Australians, Flight Sergeant Clegg and Sergeant Trigwell, had recently joined the squadron as replacement pilots.

The weather in August was generally bad and caused twenty sorties to be aborted out of a total of fifty-nine. For the first time, Group began to give alternative targets which turned out to be a good innovation and resulted in a greater number of sorties being accomplished than when there was only the one target. In addition to the aborted sorties, Agartala itself was closed on two occasions, causing scheduled sorties to be postponed.

The pattern of targets in August was much the same as in June and July, and again the Irrawaddy River was the principal area of operations. In all during August, over 700 small rivercraft were attacked and many were destroyed. In addition, a number of river steamers and barges met the same fate. It was quite apparent that the Japanese were now heavily dependent on the Irrawaddy River to move stores, equipment and men to strategic points on the river, as close as possible to where ground fighting would recommence in the Arakan and north west Burma once the monsoon ended. Other targets included oil installations along the river, whilst rail and road transport was attacked in the triangle area of Mandalay, Thazi, and Myingyan. August followed the good pattern set in July insofar as we lost no aircraft, or suffered aircrew casualties.

Once the weather improved and ground activities by both sides increased, we did not expect this pattern to continue.

Wing Commander Nicolson, VC, arrived on the morning of 4 August with his border collie dog, and in the afternoon made his first Beaufighter flight, which was suitably celebrated in the Officers Mess that evening. It was a 'getting to know you occasion' and certainly indicated the type of person our new Commanding Officer was. As is well recognised, the Victoria Cross is not achieved without an act of unusual valour on the part of the recipient, and the fact that Nicolson was the only fighter pilot of the 1939-45 war to be so decorated is indicative of the high honour he achieved, when it is considered that some twenty bomber airmen received the VC. The occasion was the

Battle of Britain and the date 16 August 1940, when the *Luftwaffe* carried out 1715 sorties against Britain. During an attack on Southern England by a large force of bombers, escorted by single and twin-engined fighters, Flight Lieutenant Nicolson, flying a Hurricane of No. 249 Squadron, was hit by cannon shells from a Messerschmitt Bf 110 fighter after losing his No. 2 and No. 3. With his cockpit on fire, his hands badly burnt, shell splinters in his left eye, and a hit to his left heel, he succeeded in shooting down a Bf 110 before baling out. Burned and wounded, his immediate reward on reaching the ground was to be shot in the buttocks by a trigger happy Local Defence Volunteer. The effects of the Battle of Britain were evident three years later when he joined No. 27 Squadron, for he could not bend his badly burnt fingers nor use his hands in the normal way – but this did not deter him from assuming the role of an active operational Commanding Officer. He remained in India until his death in 1945. In April 1983, his family auctioned his VC. The successful bidder, the RAF Battle of Britain Museum, Hendon, paid the unprecedented sum of £110,000.

August turned out to be a month of administration changes within the squadron. Apart from acquiring a new Commanding Officer, the posts of Intelligence Officer, Engineer Officer and Signals Officer underwent changes. Flying Officer Blackburn-Daniels replaced Flying Officer Wakelin; Flying Officer Allen, BEM, replaced Flying Officer Brewer, and Flying Officer Bradley replaced Flying Officer Spearing. These changes, together with that of Squadron Leader Birt who had replaced Flight Lieutenant Swift as flight commander of the 'B' Flight, gave the squadron a new look, but were carried out with a minimum of disruption to the squadron activities.

September produced better weather and out of sixty-three sorties, which was the highest monthly effort so far, only seven had to be aborted. For the third successive month, we did not lose an aircraft on operations. However, Flying Officer Ball, a navigator, was fatally wounded by small arms fire when his aircraft, piloted by Flight Lieutenant Williams, was attacking an oil barge on the Irrawaddy River near Yenanyaung. He died shortly after being admitted to Comilla Field Hospital.

The better weather apparently induced the Japanese to become more active and as a result there was increased movement on rail, river and road systems with the prime target area central Burma, followed by northern and southern Burma. In the early part of the month, the squadron chalked up its fiftieth locomotive destroyed or damaged. However, by the end of the month another twenty-six had been destroyed or damaged. Other rail targets, including freight trucks and flats, carriages – sometimes with soldiers – and signal boxes were also attacked. On the rivers the score was seven steamers/launches, thirteen barges, one vehicle ferry and 150 small rivercraft. The Japanese made much greater use of the roads in September, resulting in fifty-nine motor transports of various types being destroyed or damaged. In addition, eleven attacks were made on oil installations and fifteen on warehouse/factory type buildings. Once again, no attacks were made on aerodromes and no Japanese aircraft were sighted.

Wing Commander Nicolson must have been pleased with his squadron's performance in his first month as Commanding Officer. One 'weakness' which he apparently thought should be quickly rectified was to improve the range and quality of liquor in the Officers Mess, as a result of which I found myself with the extra assignment of Bar Officer. This entailed periodical visits to Calcutta where I first had to locate – which was not easy – and purchase at reasonable prices – again not easy – Scotch whisky, Gordon's gin, and South African brandy and sherry. I was always charged with 'and don't come back empty handed'. As part of the exercise I made it my business to also bring back whatever there was available in the way of fresh vegetables and fruit. It was generally agreed the CO had made a very good move by initiating this procedure.

It was during September that the second Beaufighter squadron, No. 177, became fully operational, and was based at nearby Fenni. As will be recalled, a number of their original aircrew had spent a little time with us at Agartala earlier in the year, where we were able to take them on our operational flights for experience.

The last month of the 1943 monsoon, October, saw a big improvement in the weather and with it greater activity by the Japanese. Out of seventy-four sorties flown, only three had to be aborted on account of bad weather. The pattern of the Japanese immediate activities became apparent to us as the month progressed and, as expected, it would be a build up of stores, equipment and men in Northern Burma, in preparation for a fresh assault into India along the Assam border, as well as a counter to the aggressive General Stilwell, who was pushing ahead with the Ledo Road towards the railhead at Myitkyina. As the month progressed, it became apparent that they would be using the railways and the remaining large river steamers to carry heavy equipment into Northern Burma and the pattern of our sorties in October confirmed that this was in fact the case.

On the two main rivers, the Irrawaddy and Chindwin, the large slow paddle-wheel steamers were constantly sought. The Japanese strategy was to sail them at night and camouflage them during the day, usually against tall river banks, when the steamers were covered with tarpaulins and tree foliage which they carried for this particular purpose. For added protection against our low-level attacks, they sometimes installed trip wires across the river which, when flying low at more than 200 mph, were very hard to pick up and were a real menace. In all, twelve river steamers were located during October, including the well known pre-war steamers, *Shwelan, Assam, Maha* and *Wuchango*. All twelve were attacked with cannon and machine gun fire and the *Shwelan* was definitely destroyed by four Beaufighters on 25 October.

On the main railway from Rangoon to Mandalay and then north to Myitkyina there was a great deal of activity. No less than thirty locomotives with their attendant passenger cars, wagons and flat tops were attacked, severely damaged and in some cases destroyed. On 19 October, the crews of Wing Commander Nicolson and Flight

Lieutenant Franklin, and Flight Sergeant Thorogood and Flying Officer Welch were detailed to 'strafe enemy communications SEDAW-GOKTEIK'. They attacked and damaged five locomotives which brought the squadron tally to one hundred since operations began eight months earlier. Thorogood and Welch were immediately sent to Calcutta where, apart from media publicity, the Group Public Relations Officer arranged for a gramophone recording to be made of the occasion for radio publicity. It was from this point that the squadron became known as the 'Train Busters'. To celebrate the occasion and notwithstanding that Ronnie T. and Edgar W. were down in Calcutta, the CO invited all aircrew to the Officers Mess for drinks.

As an indication of increased Japanese ground activity along the Burma/India border, British 4th Corps, whose headquarters were at Imphal, called for a strafing attack on 400 Japanese soldiers at Hata in the Chin Hills. Six Beaufighters were despatched to what proved to be a very difficult target, as the Japanese were in twelve basha huts in an elbow of ground 4000 feet high and 1000 feet from the top of a mountain, which meant we could not get closer than 300 yards before firing and pulling away. In all we made thirty attacks, but, although we did not see any positive effects, a couple of days later a message came through that 4th Corps were very pleased with the result. The next day, and again on the 15th, we were put on standby for similar operations, but were not called on to fly. It is opportune to mention that in September an Army Officer, Captain Pete Sanders, was attached to the squadron as Army Liaison Officer. He was an extremely likable fellow and got on very well with everyone, not objecting to being referred to by the slang Army title of 'pongo', or as 'duff gen Pete', which was based on what we thought of what he would tell us the Army were doing. He made several operational flights as observer to obtain first-hand information about selected targets, and I enjoyed his company on two of these occasions.

Apart from these major areas of activity during October, attacks were made on many small rivercraft, motor vehicles (including two staff cars), oil and water storage tanks and some buildings. No aerodromes were attacked. Another attempt was made to escort four Hurricanes into Burma, but again the speed of the Beaufighter proved too much and they turned back over the Chin Hills.

We suffered casualties on the 16th when the aircraft crewed by Sergeants Humphries and Bainton, after attacking a long train north of Toungoo, climbed to 100 feet, turned on its back and crashed to the ground. It was presumed that the aircraft – and probably the pilot – were hit by groundfire.

On the 25 October two crews, Flying Officer Mason/Flight Sergeant Shortis and Flight Sergeant Trigwell/Pilot Officer Dobson, were briefed to fly down the Kaladan River in the Arakan and return via Akyab where they were to photograph suspect military installations. Over Akyab, an explosive shell passed through the nose of Trigwell's aircraft, severely damaging the instrument panel, pieces of which entered his chest – some are still there forty years later. As well, the top of a screw lodged above his right eye, causing temporary blindness, although at the time 'Triggy' thought he was finished. He wanted to gain sufficient height for his navigator to bale out but 'Dobbie' suggested that they try to make Cox's Bazaar, 100 miles to the north. With Dobbie's help, Triggy made a low-level precautionary landing at Cox's Bazaar, scattering some 1500 workers who were carrying out runway extensions. After a couple of months Triggy was declared fit to resume flying and returned to No. 27 Squadron, where Wing Commander Nicolson, congratulated him on the effort, which included some good photographs of the military installations at Akyab. The CO told Triggy that he would like to recommend him for a Distinguished Flying Medal or a commission, to which he responded, 'In this stinking hole, I'd rather have a commission,' which was duly received. A year later, Pilot Officer Trigwell was to have an even more traumatic experience.

Two aircraft, crewed by Flying Officers Thompson and Merritt, and Flight Sergeant Clegg and Sergeant Brindstead, when operating in the Thazi-Kalaw area in Eastern Burma, were jumped by two Army 0.1 fighters. The Japanese managed three attacks, one of which resulted in Clegg's aircraft being hit in the starboard wing and engine before both aircraft escaped by superior speed. The attack made it clear that the Japanese were maintaining aircraft at the well-established He-Ho aerodrome in Eastern Burma.

At the end of October, the AOC Bengal Command, Air Vice Marshal Williams, visited the squadron and after the aircrew were paraded he said he had come to say three things:

our strafing was having a great effect on Japanese morale in Burma;

we were shortly to be re-equipped with low level Mosquitos;

Headquarters, Delhi, wished to show its appreciation of our work by making an immediate award to one crew.

A moment's pause , and when he called out Flight Sergeant Johnson, pilot, and his navigator, Flying Officer Dinwoodie, they were dumbfounded and for a few seconds neither moved. Then amidst handclapping the AOC pinned Distinguished Flying Medal and Distinguished Flying Cross ribbons on Johnny J. and Sandy D. The awards were extremely popular as both had done really good work. This of course was another reason for an aircrew celebration and when, at 1 am, the normally abstemious Sandy D. was poured into bed looking much the worse for wear, he was heard to say in his Scottish accent, 'I dinna want a bar to this DFC for a wee while yet.'

The month ended on a light note as far as I was concerned. One afternoon I received a message that the CO wanted Paddy and me at the 'drome with an overnight bag.

We reached the 'drome and were introduced by Nicolson to a general whose name I cannot recall, and his female aide-de-camp. Apparently, the daily No. 221 Group Mail Run Dakota, operated by No. 31 Squadron, which was flying them from Imphal to Calcutta had developed engine trouble, and as a result the pilot said that they could not reach Calcutta until the next day. Our job was to fly the general and his aide to Calcutta that afternoon and come back the next morning with, as the CO said to me on the side, 'some cases of booze'.

The Beaufighter was not designed to carry passengers in comfort. I seated the general as comfortably as possible in front of the cannon bins and, after the entrance hatch was closed, told the aide she would have to stand in the well created by the closed hatch, right behind me. The trip was uneventful, with the aide and I discussing topics like the weather on the way to Calcutta, where we landed at Alipore.

The general invited Paddy and me to share his car into Calcutta and either in the hurry of not keeping him waiting, or of staying to close to the aide, I overlooked putting the cover on the pitot head – the air intake that registers the air speed – which I immediately realised next morning when doing a visual aircraft inspection. Halfway down the runway, too late to stop the take-off, I checked the air speed to find it registering zero.

Once in the air I switched on the pitot head de-icing heater, hoping it might clear what must be a foreign obstruction in the pitot head, but this did not happen so I called up base as we approached Agartala, explained the situation and requested that another Beaufighter be sent up to 'talk me down'. Flying Officer Thompson was assigned to assist with the landing. This meant that I flew alongside his aircraft in the landing circuit, responding to what he said over the radio that he was doing in his aircraft, that is, reducing speed to 140 knots, flaps partly down, turning cross wind, reducing speed to 120 knots, wheels down, turning into wind, flaps fully down and reducing speed to 100 knots, after which he pulled away, and I completed the landing by the seat of my pants. With the aerodrome fire tender and ambulance moving slowly along the side of the landing strip, Paddy, in his broadest Irish brogue, said 'he wasn't very impressed'. The moral, I suppose is: 'You shouldn't mix flying with sex.' On examination, it turned out that a bee had crawled into the uncovered pitot head whilst the aircraft was parked overnight at Alipore.

Officially, the monsoon period was now over and statistically the squadron's record was pretty good. Altogether in the six months we flew 350 sorties of which seventy-four were aborted because of bad weather. Nine aircrew were lost, bringing the total to seventeen since operations began in February. The target success rate was something of which all the squadron, not just the aircrew, could be proud. As the AOC said, we were having an effect on the Japanese in Burma, which was nice to hear, considering the demands that were put on the groundstaff to keep the aircraft serviceable and on the aircrews to fly them in difficult monsoon conditions.

Most significantly, the squadron had operated through a very difficult six-month period and it was now in a position to face confidently the increasing activity that would come when the land forces of both sides locked horns in the coming months.

7·OVERCOMING JUNGLE BOREDOM

Unlike our counterparts in the United Kingdom, Dominions and Commonwealth, there was no recreation, amusement or entertainment in the sense of the English pub, cinemas or dances – Agartala was in the jungle of East Bengal, nearly 200 miles to the east of Calcutta, which was the nearest 'bright lights' centre, and until the squadron settled down, the word recreation did not mean very much. Prior to reaching Agartala, the squadron had been involved over a period of three months in two complete moves which had kept everyone so occupied there was not time to become bored – tired, yes, and sometimes frustrated, but hardly ever bored.

The overall feeling whilst we were at Amarda Road during the squadron's assembly period was one of excitement as the aircraft strength built up, and we got to know each other and the expectations about actually flying into Burma on offensive operations.

With the move to Kanchrapara, we were able to make an occasional visit to Calcutta and had temporary – albeit rather short, as already mentioned – membership of the Kanchrapara Railway Officers Club. However, it was not enough to counter the firing problems we were having with the aircraft's cannons and, for the first time since the squadron came together, there were some signs of boredom, particularly as there was an overall state of frustration over the cannon problem and the uncertainty as to where we would end up once the problem was rectified. Therefore, the CO's decision at Kanchrapara at that time to introduce a forty-eight hour leave pass system and more frequent half-days off enabled all members of the squadron to get away from the mild boredom that life on the squadron was creating.

Calcutta has always been a very crowded place and the influx of all sections of the Allied forces involved with the Burma campaign not only added to its normal congestion, but formed a climate for inter-service and inter-nationality rivalries, sometimes ending up in brawls and keeping the military police busy. Places like the Great Eastern Hotel opposite the Governor of Bengal's Palace, the Grand Hotel and Firpo's Restaurant on Chowringhee were natural gathering points, and it was not hard for all facets of the Allied forces – army, navy, air force, whether British or American –

to become argumentatively involved with one another in determining what each was doing there and who was winning the war.

Chowringhee was one of the main streets of Calcutta with commercial buildings and shops, including the Grand Hotel and Firpo's Restaurant, occupying the southern side. On the other side was a large park known as the Maidan and through it ran a road, known as Red Road, which had been turned into a runway for fighter aircraft and was in constant use. Sitting on a balcony of the Grand Hotel sipping a local Murree beer, watching the Hurricanes take-off and land, was regarded as a form of 'entertainment'. I did not think then that I would one day land an aeroplane on Red Road, but it did happen in 1944 after I had left No. 27 Squadron. With my No. 27 Squadron navigator, Paddy, we were conducting an enquiry into the crash of a Hurricane which had been flying from Allahabad to Calcutta, killing the pilot, for which purpose I was flying a Fairchild Argus. We got quite a kick out of landing on Red Road, checking in, then walking across Chowringhee to an old stamping ground, The Grand Hotel, for a drink.

Shopping for tropical clothing and personal items was another form of 'entertainment' on the occasional visits to Calcutta, as it inevitably involved haggling over prices with the astute Indian shopkeepers. There were occasional race meetings at the Turf Club which some members of the squadron managed to attend.

Once it was known that our operational base was to be Agartala, Wing Commander Daish had been quick to realise that squadron personnel were likely to face boredom after they settled down there to routine duties, and he was responsible, soon after we arrived, for setting up discussion groups, lectures and a soccer competition. A lecture room was made available for those interested in forming discussion groups, as well as for those who wished to attend advertised lectures, under the control of Flight Lieutenant Franklin, the CO's navigator. The discussion groups covered such topics as Post War Planning, Women in the Post War World, The Beveridge Plan, and Automobile Engineering.

The lectures were varied – one of the most popular series attended by airmen were subjects relating to aircrew qualifications and no doubt those attending had in mind to apply for a transfer to flying duties. Subjects included mathematics, navigation and morse code, and the instructors were Franklin and Sergeant Parker. Learning the local language was initially popular as there was an obvious advantage in being able to understand and use common words and phrases, such as *ek, do, tien* (one, two, three), *tanda pani* (cold water), *gharam cha* (hot tea), *chota* (little) etc. The lecturer, Lieutenant Wells, was an Army officer based at Agartala. By contrast, an attempt to introduce a French language class by Warrant Officer Rowe, who was in charge of squadron discipline, was not at all popular.

There were lectures for the aircrew about Burma and the Burmese, given by Squadron Leader O'Leary from Group HQ and Colonel Hodgkinson from inter-service Public Relations Group HQ. We did not attempt to learn Burmese as it is not an easy language to master and the only time we would require it would be if we crash landed in Burma and needed to communicate with the local people. To some degree this was taken care of in a pamphlet of phrases included with a survival kit issued to aircrew before they went on operations. One of the phrases was 'I want a guide to take me to . . .', which in Burmese reads: *'thwa bo, lan pya low gyin deh. . .'*.

The inter-squadron – and later inter-unit – soccer competitions, under the control of Flying Officer Cotter, were very popular, but, because of the heat, we only played twenty-minute halves and on a shortened ground. The inter-squadron competition was for the CO's trophy, the Daish Cup, and, in 1943, two competitions were held, with the aircrew team winning the first and the headquarters team winning the second. The games were played at 5 o'clock in the afternoon and, by the time they were finished, all were in a lather of perspiration, including the author who was the goalkeeper for the aircrew team, and, fortunately for him, had less running to do than those out on the field. The Daish Cup is still part of No. 27 Squadron records and is 'somewhere in England'.

Other popular forms of sport were archery and badminton. However, what many of us missed was somewhere to swim. The word Bengal is sometimes linked to the word tiger, and whilst we sometimes heard from the locals that there was a tiger in the vicinity, or of one being killed, squadron personnel never came across one. However, towards the end of 1943, pigeon shooting became a popular sport and resulted in some good bags being taken.

There was a station open air cinema which was well patronised by all units in Agartala. The screenings were usually films of the 1930s, and on a clear starry night it was a pleasant way to spend a couple of hours, notwithstanding that you may already have seen the film. On one occasion, an Indian circus visited Agartala and the Indian strongman invited sixteen airmen to have a tug of war, with himself between two teams of eight and with the rope passing around his neck. He had to protect his neck by using his arms to take the pull of each team, but he sadly underestimated the muscle power of sixteen airmen, and it took some time before he revived from near strangulation.

Another of the circus's acts was the two-piece orchestra of trombone player and drummer who drove everybody mad by playing at every opportunity 'She had to go and lose it at the Astor'. In October, a squadron concert was held when anyone who had talent could participate – a couple of skits, 'St Peter in Heaven' and '27 Squadron, 27 Men' were very popular acts.

No. 27 Squadron had left Agartala before an ENSA concert party arrived, which included Vera Lynn, who was the first white woman some of the airmen at Agartala had seen for nearly two years. A story goes that there was a queuing up for Vera's autograph during which the officer in charge made a remark which caused much laughter: 'There's no need to push, you'll all get what you want.'

The officers were privileged in December to be invited by the Maharajah of Tripura to Ujjayanta Palace for a concert and supper. It was a very colourful affair with Indian artists performing local dances such as Snake Charmer, Fire Dance and Miser's Wealth.

We were guests, and sometimes hosts, for dinner of the other squadrons at Agartala – the most rowdy and boisterous was a visit to No. 17 Squadron. As the night wore on, the challenge to a game of saddle-me-nag inevitably arose, and its main purpose, from No. 17 Squadron's point of view, was to push down the end of their mess once more. The sheer weight of those present ultimately caused the wall to collapse and with it, of course, some forty to fifty men. Eventually, one of the members broke an arm and that put finis to the game.

At night, squadron personnel developed their own interests – reading, writing, laundry, playing cards or darts, or just sitting around talking. In the officers mess there was a gramophone which had to compete with one owned by Flight Lieutenant Swift, which he kept in his quarters and churned out 'Dearly Beloved' every night. Wing Commander Nicolson was a liar dice addict and to get involved with him meant several hours of play with losers buying drinks. Dedicated card players concentrated on contract bridge and the same four would play for a week before there was a settling. Another card game that was quite popular was a form of patience called 'racing demons'.

Animal pets were very much a part of the Agartala scene and they provided company, fun and entertainment, not only to their owners, but other members of the squadron. Flight Lieutenant Swift arrived with Tikton – or Tiki as he was generally called, and on special occasions Air Rajah Dog Tikton. He was an English wire-haired terrier, which Swift first flew from England to the Middle East and then to India. After Tiki died, Flight Lieutenants Swift and Franklin arrived back from leave in Calcutta with two dachshund pups which they rather appropriately called Schmidt and Goering.

Although dogs and monkeys were the most popular pets, two Himalayan bears became a real feature. They were acquired as cubs by Pilot Officer John Townsend while the squadron was forming up at Amarda Road in December 1942, when they were five weeks old and could be held in the palms of Townsend's hands. They were called Elsie and Rupert. After John was lost on operations on 17 February 1943, Flight Lieutenant Horn, later assisted by Flying Officer Williams, took over their raising, which included construction of a strong bamboo shelter for sleeping and protection against the weather. They were kept on long leads which allowed them to feed on natural foliage and, in particular, bamboo shoots, which grew prolifically around the officers' compound. This natural food was supplemented with vegetable scraps from the kitchen and powdered milk, which suited their palate, for in less than one year they were nearly four feet tall and weighed over one hundred pounds. 'Bunny' Horn lost control over them when the mating season arrived and sadly it was decided that one of them would have to be shot, because, if they became loose, they were very likely to attack any person who tried to get near them. It was a sad day when Elsie was shot.

Apart form my own Modu, 'Snow' Swift and 'Chiefy' Salter, who was the 'B' Flight Flight Sergeant Engineer, also acquired rhesus monkeys. One of the highlights of late afternoon entertainment in the officers compound was when Modu, on a long lead, was tied to a charpoy bed. 'Bunny' Horn would bring along Elsie and Rupert who were loose, and the three animals would then engage in an hilarious rough and tumble over, under and around the charpoy.

The adjutant, Joe Talbot, acquired a mongoose whilst a Dalmatian dog attached itself to one of the groundcrew – where it came from no-one seemed to know.

After we had settled into Agartala, news came out that aircrew were to have two weeks leave every three months and groundcrew two weeks leave every six months, it being compulsory to leave the station. This was to provide a break from the unpleasant weather conditions, and for it to be effective, we were expected to head for the cooler mountain areas. The groundcrew had Hill Station facilities provided to the north of Agartala at Shillong in Assam, whilst most aircrew headed for Darjeeling ('place of thunderbolt'), in the Himalayas. As would be expected, a few headed for the fleshpots of Calcutta.

Darjeeling, regarded as 'Queen of the Hill Stations', some 400 miles to the north of Calcutta at an altitude of over 6500 feet and a minimum/maximum temperature range of thirty-five/sixty degrees Fahrenheit, provided welcome relief from the tiring Agartala climate. To get there we flew to Calcutta, took an overnight train to Siliguri at the foot of the Himalayas, transferring to a taxi, or to the British built two-foot narrow gauge train with its four complete loops and five switchbacks to counteract gradients as much as one in twenty. The taxi took about one and a half hours and the train – which is still operating – about six hours to climb the fifty miles to Darjeeling. Across the valley to the north, and nearly always in view, was the magnificent Mount Kanchenjunga (28,146 feet), the world's third highest mountain. Mount Everest (29,028 feet) could be seen very early in the morning 125 miles to the west from the top of nearby Tiger Hill, provided the weather was clear.

We usually stayed at the Hotel Darjeeling or the Windemere Hotel and were made welcome at the Planters Club and the Gymkhana Club. The Planters Club, as the name implies, was the meeting place of the expatriate (usually English) tea planters, the last of whom, Geoffrey J. Ower-Johnson, was murdered on his estate in April 1981 by the workers at his factory. The Gymkhana Club provided sporting facilities, including tennis, squash, billiards, as well as controlling the racecourse at Lebong, 1000 feet below Darjeeling. A day at the Lebong Races was an experience. It was said to be the highest and smallest racecourse in the world –.so small, in fact, that after the horses had made a pre-determined number of circuits of the course the barriers were realigned for the final lap, so that there was a 'straight' which was in effect the main street of Lebong village. It was also said to be the crookedest but, no doubt, there are other racecourses in the world that could equally fit this description.

Darjeeling was a popular holiday centre for British people who were employed in many parts of India and many friendships between servicemen and locally employed Europeans were established as a result of meetings at Darjeeling. I became associated with the McKay family, Bill, Molly and their young daughter, Shirley. Bill managed the India Jute Mills at Serampore, ten miles north of Calcutta on the Hooghly River, where I and other members of the squadron were always welcome. Darjeeling became a popular place to spend a leave and it was not surprising to find that it was soon referred to as 'Gee Darling'.

Other leave experiments were tried. Just as there were large passenger river steamers with accommodation plying the Irrawaddy and Chindwin Rivers of Burma, so were there large passenger steamers plying the Indian rivers, with Calcutta as the central point. One such service operated from the nearby Meghna River, which joined the Ganges River and eventually reached Calcutta through a maze of waterways that make up the mouths of the Ganges. It was used on one leave occasion by Flight Lieutenant Swift, who described it as an interesting experience. As the Japanese had not developed No. 27 Squadron's strategy of strafing river steamers, the Indian rivers were certainly safer to travel than their Burma counterparts the Irrawaddy and Chindwin.

Another leave experiment was made by my navigator, Paddy, and myself, who decided to visit Kashmir. To get there and back involved six days of travel, first by train from Calcutta to Rawalpindi in north-west India, then a hair-raising ride by local bus to the capital of Kashmir, Srinagar, which included an overnight stop at Murree where Indian beer was brewed. However, the week spent on a houseboat on Dal Lake, 6,500 feet high and surrounded by the most magnificent snow-covered mountains, certainly compensated for the long journey from Agartala and was well worth the effort. We swam, successfully fished for trout in the wild fast-running Jhelum River, went for escorted mountain hikes, and had local meals cooked by our friendly houseboat owner.

Both Darjeeling and Srinagar are places I would very much like to re-visit.

8·AFTER THE 1943 MONSOON

The weather throughout November was good and no sorties were aborted. During the month, sixty-five sorties were carried out, mainly against rail, road and river communications in Central and Northern Burma. Not only were the Japanese very active in moving supplies into Northern Burma, but their ground fire was more aggressive than during the monsoon months, and three Beaufighters and their crews were lost as a result of ground fire. Flight Lieutenant Williams, with his navigator, Flying Officer Herbert, managed to crash land near Tangon in Northern Burma, only to be captured by the Japanese. Shortly after their loss, a Captain Herbert of the British Army arrived unannounced to meet up with brother Ken, only to learn that his aircraft had just recently crash landed in Burma, but he was told by the crew of the second aircraft, Flight Sergeant Tosh and Sergeant Waite, that they had reason to believe the crew were alive. It was subsequently learnt that Williams and Herbert died as a result of a hunger strike following a rebellion by the PoW's in a Rangoon prison, known as the Ritz, when a guard was killed.

The tally for the month included twenty-two locomotives, thirteen motor transports, three armoured cars and twenty river steamers, launches, barges and sampans. On two occasions, groups of army tanks were attacked; one group was loaded on open-top rail-cars at Kume Road and suffered severe damage from the 20 mm cannons of my Beaufighter. To the east of Kume Road in the Shan Hills, a Japanese army camp at Taunggyyi was strafed twenty-four times by two Beaufighters. One unpleasant operation involving attacks on Burmese bullock carts was carried out on roads west of the Chindwin River that led into the Chin and Naga Hills where the Japanese were building up their forces for the expected attack on north-east India. All the bullock carts travelling north were heavily loaded and those travelling south were empty, indicating that the Burmese were probably being forced by the Japanese to carry out these dangerous transportation activities. It was in this area that another group of armoured tanks, this time on the ground, were attacked. Both Beaufighter crews who carried out the attack were of the opinion they were British tanks and, if so, they would have been among those abandoned during the British evacuation eighteen months earlier.

In the casualty area, apart from the crash landing in Burma by Williams and Herbert, two Beaufighters were shot down as a result of heavy ground fire. At the Ywatung South aerodrome, Flying Officer Hassell's aircraft was hit in both engines by Bofors type ack-ack – he managed to fly about sixty miles before the aircraft spun in and burst into flames, killing both of the crew, Hassell and Flight Sergeant Thomas. Whilst attacking three armoured cars between Kume Road and Thazi, Sergeant Plummer's aircraft was hit, causing it to crash immediately and burst into flames, killing both of the crew, Sergeants Plummer and Collingwood. On a more fortunate note, the Beaufighters of Sergeant Johnson, DFM, and Flight Sergeant Vincent were both severely damaged whilst attacking motor transports at Padaung. Johnson's aircraft lost the pressure in its brake system, which resulted in a crash landing back at Agartala, while his navigator, Flying Officer Dinwoodie, DFC, had the heels of both boots blown away. The rudder of Vincent's aircraft was damaged making flying very difficult, but he was able to get back to Agartala where he made a very skilful landing.

During the month Squadron Leader Hallett, No. 224 Group Intelligence Officer, Flight Lieutenant Blackburn-Daniels, the No. 27 Squadron Intelligence Officer, and Group Captain Champion de Crespigny, the station commanding officer, made operational sorties with the squadron as observers. The new AOC Bengal Command, Air Marshal Sir John Baldwin, KBE, CB, DSO, visited the squadron and, not to be outdone, the Japanese made a bombing raid on 29 November, causing some minor damage to the runway and forcing two Beaufighters that were out on operations to be diverted to Comilla and Chittagong.

The good weather, which was pleasantly cool in the evenings, continued through December. The number of sorties carried out during the month, eighty-six, was the highest monthly total since the squadron began operations. One aircraft with its crew of Flight Sergeant Vincent and Sergeant Mathewson, who had not long joined the squadron, were lost in unusual circumstances. Flying as number two to Wing Commander Nicolson the two aircraft were approaching the Irrawaddy River south of Padan when Vincent's aircraft suddenly turned away and headed north and was not seen again. It can only be assumed that it was hit by ground fire.

In regard to the conduct of the war in Burma, there were two important developments towards the end of 1943. The most significant took place on 16 November, when Rear-Admiral Lord Louis Mountbatten, GC, VO, CB, DSO, ADC, became Supreme Allied Commander in South East Asia. However, the change which most directly affected our operations took place a month later, on 16 December, when Air Headquarters, Bengal, which had moved from Barrackpore near Calcutta to Comilla, East Bengal, was reconstituted as Third Tactical Air Force, remaining under the command of Air Marshal Sir John Baldwin, who became Air Marshal commanding Third Tactical Air Force.

The squadron's activities were increasingly inseparable from what the Allied and

Japanese armies were doing in the Arakan, in the north-eastern area of the Naga Hills and in Northern Burma. In the Arakan, the British 15th Corps, comprising three Divisions, went on the offensive with the objective of re-capturing Akyab. It was opposed to the Japanese 28th Army. In the north-eastern area of the Naga Hills, the Japanese strategy was for its 15th Army to seize Kohima, the mountain gateway to India, a strategy which had top Japanese priority. The 15th Army was opposed to the British 4th Corps. Further to the north, General Stilwell's Northern Area Combat Command, which was based at Ledo, had as its objective the capture of the key Burmese town of Myitkyina. It was opposed to the Japanese 18th Division. As it turned out, the Japanese activity in the Arakan was of a diversionary nature – although it had the appearance of an invasion of Bengal – and their primary objective was the capture of Kohima in north-eastern India. Much has been written about both campaigns – in particular, how, under General (later Field Marshal) Slim's direction, the British troops, when cut off by the Japanese encircling tactics in the Arakan, stayed put and fought, relying upon the air for supplies. The success of this tactic is now history. In the same way, 'the seige of Kohima' is legendary; had it been lost by the Allies, the Japanese would have been given a very significant victory in the early months of 1944.

It was therefore not surprising that more than half of the squadron's sorties in December were flown in the Arakan and the remainder almost entirely in central and southern Burma. Again, Japanese lines of communication were the prime targets, and this resulted in the destruction of or damage to twenty-four locomotives, some hundreds of rail trucks, over one hundred road transports, eleven river steamers, seven barges and many small rivercraft. In addition, five oil/water storage tanks, an army barracks, a power house and several warehouse structures were attacked.

On one operation in the Arakan, during December involving my aircraft and that of Flight Sergeant Thorogood, it was noticed that extensive defence work was being carried out along the beaches on Ramree Island – no doubt in expectation of an Allied landing. We ran into considerable small arms fire – one bullet bursting the water bottle behind my navigator's legs. Another bullet hit the port hydraulics of Thorogood's aircraft, rendering the undercarriage unserviceable as a result of which he flew back to the Kanchrapara Maintenance Unit, where he made a successful belly landing, for which effort he was given a 'green endorsement'.

Following the discovery of these beach defences on Ramree Island, four Beaufighters were sent to attack them, as well as any Japanese who showed their presence, and at the same time the Army requested as much information as possible on the structure of the defences. Consequently, Captain Sanders, the Army Liaison Officer attached to the squadron, flew with me as an observer in the Beaufighter that had been specially fitted with the fourteen-inch camera, which had been nicknamed *'Chota Beau Dekko'*, or, in English, *'Little Bo Peep'*. The camera worked beautifully, and we got some very detailed pictures of the defences. Unfortunately, Squadron Leader Birt, who was leading the attack, was hit on the left hand by an explosive bullet, but with the aid of his navigator, Flight Sergeant Jones, was able to make a safe landing at Cox's Bazaar. Birt lost three fingers and never returned to the squadron, where he had been the 'B' Flight Commander for the previous three months.

Early in the month, following a signal from Group Headquarters, I took a detachment of five Beaufighters to Chittagong for special sea convoy duties over the next three days. It turned out that the Army were bringing a number of fully-loaded tank landing barges from Calcutta for a landing down the Mayu Peninsular, where the 15th Corps were engaged, and our job was to provide daylight cover against possible Japanese aircraft attacks. The closest we got to action was a signal from Group on the first day which read '100 + aircraft approaching from the south-east'. We never saw these aircraft, which passed over the convoy at about 25,000 feet on their way to bomb Calcutta, but it did prompt Flying Officer Cross to remark, 'here comes some posthumous gongs'. In all, we provided sixty-four hours of escort duties and, hopefully, gave the Navy and Army some comfort by our presence. With so many officers away on this operation, the Officers Mess was reduced to thirteen for dinner, whereupon Wing Commander Nicolson invited the Mess Corporal Weir to join them for dinner.

December saw the beginning of night operations and altogether seventeen night sorties were flown. It was a new experience to strafe low-level in the dark. Operations were confined to moonlight nights, with, hopefully, no ground fogs, as these conditions would give us the best chance of identifying and attacking targets. Twelve of the sorties were over the Taungup Pass, which was being used by the Japanese at night to send men and supplies by road convoys from Prome to the Arakan. As soon as an attack was made, the motor vehicle lights would be extinguished, and it then became impossible to continue the attacks in this mountainous region; in all, twenty motor vehicles were attacked in the first month of night attacks. Five locomotives were also attacked and this new threat to the Japanese lines of communication undoubtedly caused them more headaches.

Throughout the month, 'B' Flight had been kept very busy flying Beaufighters on operations, whilst 'A' Flight was converting to Mosquitos. The day arrived when the Mosquitos flown by No. 27 Squadron's own aircrews were ready for operations. On Christmas Day 1943 – exactly one year to the day since the first Beaufighter went into operational service in Burma – the CO, Nicolson, with Flight Lieutenant Franklin as navigator, accompanied by his number two Flying Officer Thompson and Sergeant Chippendale as navigator, attacked rail and road communications in Central Burma, inflicting much damage on two locomotives, many rail trucks and one motor vehicle. One further operation was carried out by the Mosquitos before the month ended, resulting in two locomotives, several rail trucks and some rivercraft in southern Burma being severely damaged.

On 16 December, the squadron was given a special assignment. Squadron Leader

Horn, the 'A' Flight Commander, had the privilege of flying, in a Mosquito, the supreme Allied Commander South East Asia, Mountbatten, on a tour of inspection over the Arakan front lines. The Mosquito was escorted by Spitfires of No. 615 Squadron, RAF.

Traditionally, the officers and NCOs served the other ranks with their 1943 Christmas Dinner. In the course of having our own celebrations, Wing Commander Nicolson had a fall which resulted in a broken wrist!

As 1943 came to an end, we were hearing reports about the construction of a 250-mile railway by Allied prisoners of war through the jungles of southern Burma which, when completed, would provide the Japanese in Burma with a major rail link with their base in Siam and would obviate the need to send supply ships to Rangoon via Singapore. The railway, which was commenced in October 1942, was operative by early 1944, costing the lives of some 13,000 Allied prisoners of war and an estimated 90,000 native workers. Much has been written about the infamous Siam-Burma Death Railway and, whilst there were some bombing attacks on it in 1943 by Wellingtons from India, any bombing success was tied to the likelihood of killing Allied prisoners of war and native workers; as a result, they were not maintained. Having the railway operative early in 1944 allowed the Japanese to strengthen their Burma lines of communication and would mean more rail, road and river targets for No. 27 Squadron's Beaufighters and Mosquitos.

The weather in the first two weeks of January 1944 was not good for low-level attacks. Two sorties were aborted. There was much cloud over the mountains and fog in the valleys, and Agartala was closed for flying for two days because of continuous heavy rain.

Notwithstanding the poor weather in the early part of January, the squadron flew sixty-two sorties during the whole month, of which sixteen were by Mosquitos and forty-six by Beaufighters, including nine at night. The main target areas were Central and Northern Burma. On the rivers, more than 200 steamers, barges, launches and other supply carrying craft were attacked; on the railways, fifteen locomotives and fifty-seven rail-trucks were destroyed or damaged. Motor vehicle targets included thirty lorries, three buses, two staff cars and two bullock cart convoys, whilst fourteen oil or water storage tanks and seventeen buildings comprising army barracks, warehouses, pumping stations, locomotive sheds and sawmills came under attack. Our losses were two Beaufighters and their crews. Flight Sergeant Britter, with his navigator, Flight Sergeant Paine, were hit by ground-fire east of Taungup, causing their Beaufighter to crash immediately and burst into flames. On a night sortie, Pilot Officer Gunn, with his navigator, Flight Sergeant Luff, became the first Mosquito casualty when, in moutainous country through which the Chindwin River flows north of Monywa, and with the moon hidden by cloud, the aircraft flew into the ground. In addition, two aircraft returning from operations added to the aircraft casualty list. Squadron Leader

Horn lost his air pressure system and, without brakes, the Beaufighter finished in a ditch – I had had the same experience in the Middle East, only my Beaufighter, as it came to the end of its landing run, did a ground loop, causing the left undercarriage to collapse. The second aircraft casualty was Flight Sergeant Sewell's Beaufighter, which he had to crash land at Agartala when his undercarriage would not come down.

The introduction of the Mosquitos to the squadron's operational activities meant that targets further afield could now be attacked. The most distant operation was by Flight Lieutenant Torrance, who, with his navigator, Flight Sergeant Shortis, on 13 January strafed communications from Pegu, east of Rangoon, to Moulmein – a return journey from Cox's Bazaar in the Arakan, where the aircraft had refuelled before setting out, of some 1200 miles. By contrast, the Beaufighters' longest operations were about 900 miles to places such as Lashio in Northern Burma, Ywathit in Eastern Burma and Bassein in Southern Burma.

Word came through on 7 January that the CO's navigator, Flight Lieutenant Franklin, had been awarded the Distinguished Flying Cross. 'Frankie' was popular with everyone and the award was duly celebrated with another mess party. Very soon word drifted back to the squadron that Flight Lieutenant Swift, 'B' Flight Commander until the end of August, and now a Controller at Combined War Room Operations, Colombo, had also been awarded the Distinguished Flying Cross, which was linked to the good work he had also done with No. 272 (Beaufighter) Squadron in the Middle East, prior to joining No. 27 Squadron.

On 31 December, a Wing Commander Winfield, AFC, arrived at the squadron and stayed for a few days, during which time he made two operational flights as an observer with Nicolson and Franklin. We had become used to visits from top ranking RAF and Army officers and 'another wing commander' did not make much of an impression at the time. However, the reason for his visit came as a surprise to me when I read his book *The Sky Belongs To Them*, which was completed by others following his death in 1970. He had made such strong reference to No. 27 Squadron that I would be remiss – and I am sure the reader will agree – if I did not repeat some of the comments he had to make, in particular about Wing Commander Nicolson, the Commanding Officer.

First, about Wing Commander Roland Winfield, AFC, himself. He had joined the RAF in June 1939 as a medical officer, but, after being evacuated from France in 1940, he qualified as a pilot, taking a particular interest in the problems of flying personnel. His aeromedical reports quickly attracted the notice of the Medical Directorate-General and, in November 1940, he was appointed chief assistant to the RAF Consultant in Applied Physiology, Royal Aircraft Establishment, Farnborough. The stress of war was his chosen study, and, at his request, he was authorised to fly on war operations for the stated purpose of assessing aeromedical problems at first hand.

His research into the problems facing aircrews on operational duties was almost unlimited. It covered subjects including airsickness, extreme cold, fatigue, sleep-wakefulness, oxygen starvation, searchlight dazzle, flying clothing, dingies, seat harness, crash stations and the injuries of parachutists. He made it a practice to take an active part in experiments, for example, in decompression sickness or the extension of the limits of the oxygen system. He was the first live subject in the RAF to try the 'snatch' concept, which became the procedure for picking up agents behind the enemy lines by an aircraft flying low and slow catching a cable attached to the agent.

He had medical charge of Prime Minister Churchill on his flights to Teheran and Moscow and back to London. He flew against the enemy the equivalent of three normal tours of operational duties and was awarded the Air Force Cross in 1942 and the Distinguished Flying Cross in 1944, whilst, towards the end of the war, the Air Ministry allocated him a personal aircraft – an unusual recognition for a wing commander, especially one of the medical branch.

The objective of everyone who worked at Farnborough's Physiology Laboratory was to improve the lot of men who flew, particularly the working conditions of aircrew on a day to day basis, through to how long they should be overseas. It was in this role that Wing Commander Winfield made his brief visit to No. 27 Squadron, although the reasons were not made known to the aircrew at the time.

In his book he wrote, ' 7 Squadron and 27 Squadron were the two finest squadrons I ever flew on operations with, finest because they were the most deadly instruments of war.' High praise indeed when a great many squadrons carried out so many dangerous and arduous duties throughout the world. No. 7 Squadron flew Sterlings from Oakington in Cambridgeshire and was under the command of Wing Commander H. R. Graham, DSO. Winfield devoted a chapter to No. 27 Squadron, which he entitled 'Nicolson and the Beaufighters'. I can do no better than borrow some of the comments he made.

I admired Nicolson because he had moulded his squadron into the finest instrument of war I came across in India and because of the way he had done it. He had achieved his object by inspiring a loyalty in the members of the squadron he commanded through the example he set them; and the discipline that is born from loyalty to leadership of this kind is the highest form of discipline that exists. He never asked any crew to make a sortie against the Japanese that was as dangerous as the sortie he chose for himself; and he not only reserved the most hazardous flights for his own execution, but made a point of flying more often on operations than any other crew on squadron.

27 Squadron was unique in the whole of my experience in India, and I admired Nicolson even more when I discovered what it was that had driven him first to create and then to command its spirit of complete operational efficiency. He was haunted by the doubt of whether or not he was really worth the Victoria Cross he had won. He said to me, 'Doc. I shall never know if I should have done what I did if I'd had the time to weigh up the pros and cons in cold blood. If you're given a decoration that you cannot refuse and yet are not sure that you've deserved, then the only thing to do is shape your life so that what's left of it is an honest attempt to show yourself and the rest of the RAF that at least you've tried to earn it.'

Nicholson proved beyond a shadow of doubt that he was worth his Victoria Cross, and that he deserved a Bar to this decoration for the manner which he commanded 27 Squadron is one of my most firmly held beliefs.

Nicolson with his squadron navigation officer, Franklin, made up the crew of a Beaufighter and the result of this combination was a mixture of initiative, skill and wisdom that made up the most formidable aircrew I ever flew with.

Neither Nicolson nor Franklin survived the Burma Campaign; having got to know them both very well, I can hear them saying, had they done so, 'Doc, we only did what had to be done'. For my part, and I'm sure every other member of No. 27 Squadron who served under the wing commander, I found him to be a person with a pleasant, outgoing, friendly nature, that made you feel comfortable and relaxed when in his presence, and probably it was this attribute that generated the best out of those who served with him. I might add the determination described by Winfield in relation to the operational sorties he shared with Nicolson was just as evident in the many games of liar dice some of us shared with him in the mess after dinner. But there is one point which I feel should be raised.

Wing Commander Nicolson had joined No. 27 Squadron five months earlier, in August. By then the squadron, under Wing Commander Daish, had been established eight months and had gone through teething troubles which any new squadron in strange surroundings could expect to experience. It would be fair to say that the squadron, when Wing Commander Daish handed it over to Nicolson, was in good shape, especially in regard to morale and the successful job it was doing against the Japanese. So it might be said, without detracting from Winfield's comments, that Nicolson took over the squadron when it had already begun to show its mettle as a successful low-level attack fighter squadron. I do not have any doubt that, were he alive, Nicolson would agree with this view.

On 22 January, Squadron Leader Bassingthwaighte, DFC – or as he was generally known, 'B16', because of the number of letters in his name – arrived at Agartala to take over 'B' Flight from Squadron Leader Birt, who had not returned to the squadron following the injuries he had incurred from Japanese ground fire over Ramree Island in December. B16 had not flown a Beaufighter before, and, being a fellow Australian, I was detailed by Nicolson to give him a familiarisation flight before he went solo. The CO probably thought that it was logical to put two Australians together for the operation. As mentioned earlier, B16 had operated against the Japanese with No. 113 (Blenheim) Squadron from January 1942 to February 1943, completing fifty-seven sorties, and had been the first Australian in the Burma theatre of war to receive the Distinguished Flying Cross.

B16 developed a love for the Beaufighter which was reflected in his life in later years. His family owned the well-known Woodlands cattle property at Greenmount in

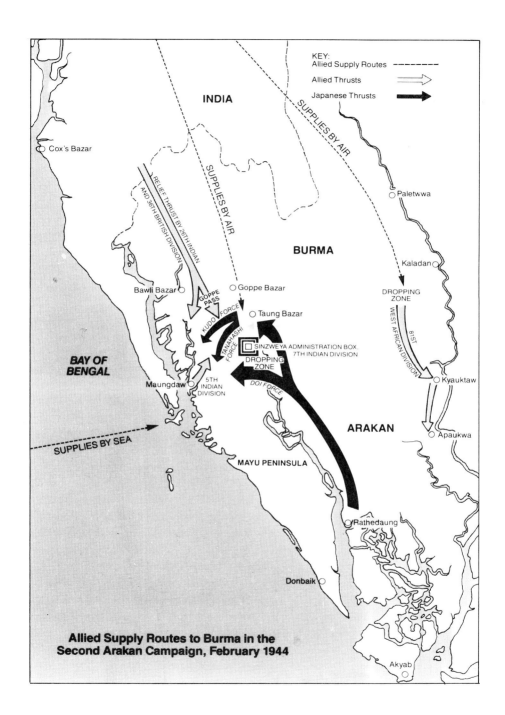

KEY:
Allied Supply Routes ---------
Allied Thrusts ⇨
Japanese Thrusts ➡

INDIA

Cox's Bazar

SUPPLIES BY AIR

SUPPLIES BY AIR

RELIEF THRUST BY 26TH INDIAN AND 36TH BRITISH DIVISION

Bawli Bazar

GOPPE PASS

KUDO FORCE

Goppe Bazar

Taung Bazar

BURMA

Paletwwa

Kaladan

DROPPING ZONE

WEST AFRICAN DIVISION

81ST

SINZWEYA ADMINISTRATION BOX.
7TH INDIAN DIVISION

BAY OF BENGAL

TANAHASHI FORCE

DROPPING ZONE

Maungdaw

5TH INDIAN DIVISION

DOI FORCE

Kyauktaw

ARAKAN

SUPPLIES BY SEA

Apaukwa

MAYU PENINSULA

Rathedaung

Donbaik

**Allied Supply Routes to Burma in the
Second Arakan Campaign, February 1944**

Akyab

89

southern Queensland, Australia, and when he returned to the land after the war, he vowed when something special in a stud animal came along he would call it Woodlands Beaufighter. During the 1960s, he finally bred a Poll Hereford bull that met his criteria and at the Brisbane Royal Show in August 1968, it won the under twenty-one month's class, the senior and grand championship for its superb scale, quality and hindquarters. Beacause Woodlands Beaufighter's sire Calliope Kingsley was still a young bull, there was no place at Woodlands for Beaufighter, so B16 sold him to the famous Jenerwarra Stud in Western Australia, who wanted the best Poll Hereford bull that money could buy and, in fact, paid a record 25,000 Australian Dollars. It is unfortunate that in recent year's B16's health has been far from good, and for some time now he has been confined to bed.

February 1944 was the squadron's most active flying month since its formation fifteen months earlier; the weather was good, no operations had to be aborted and there were no fatalities. In all, there were fifty-four separate operations, of which twenty-two were at night. Of the ninety-one aircraft involved, nineteen were Mosquitos. Road, river and rail communications were the main targets and, in line with Army activities, most of the operations were in the Arakan and Northern Burma.

The targets that were attacked and destroyed or damaged on the roads, included eighteen motor vehicles, some of which were carrying troops and oil, one tank, three staff cars, two buses and, sadly for those of us who were involved, more than 500 bullock carts. On the rivers, the score was three steamers, five launches, four barges, and between 700 and 800 small river craft which were being used by the Japanese to carry military supplies in the same manner as they were doing with the bullock carts.

Attacks on rail transport included those on twenty-five locomotives, some of which were in underground shelters – a new ploy by the Japanese to protect them from daylight attacks, thus restricting their use to the hours of darkness to a considerable extent. In addition, at least 200 rail trucks were attacked, some carrying troops, supplies and motor vehicles on flat top rail cars and, for the first time, two 250 pound bombs were fitted to the Beaufighters and were used to bomb railway bridges. Attacks on ground installations included factories, warehouses, barracks, a power house, an oil pipeline that was set on fire in three places, a power line and thirteen storage tanks – twelve holding water and one oil.

Many of the night operations were made to the old familiar Taungup Pass – from Prome to Taungup. Again our targets were motor vehicles with their lights on, heading for the Arakan with troops and supplies, which was always a difficult exercise because of the mountainous nature of the terrain. At best, only one attack could be made on a vehicle or convoy as, once alerted to our presence, the drivers obviously doused their lights. Group Headquarters must have sensed that we were getting frustrated with this particular activity, especially when we sometimes returned after four and a half hours' flying to report that nothing had been seen, or at the best only one attack had been made.

A message came through from Group to inform us that 'no targets sighted' meant that the Japanese movements were being hindered and that the Army were satisfied with our performance.

In February, I was returning from one operation to Agartala over the sea past Ramree Island in the early morning hours of darkness when the sky to the west over the Bay of Bengal suddenly opened up with heavy naval gunfire which my navigator, Paddy, and I could only guess were shells on their way to the island, and which probably had something to do with the fortifications of the beaches on the island which we had first sighted and photographed in December. I promptly dropped height down to just above sea-level and increased speed to get away from a rather unhealthy area.

Two attacks were made during February on the aerodromes at Toungoo and He-Ho. The attack on Toungoo was made at night by one Mosquito, the second having returned to Agartala with engine trouble. It was a moonlight night enabling Flying Officer C. S. Emeny, a New Zealander who had recently joined the squadron, to strafe aircraft pens and buildings, but he was not able to gauge the extent of damage caused. (Emeny, when operating later with another squadron, was taken a prisoner of war after crash landing in Burma. He survived, but had to endure being made to stand erect for five days and nights, bashings and questioning about his unit and the performance of the Mosquito.)

The attack on He-Ho was more exciting, involving four Beaufighters, including the author's, and was led by Nicolson. We were to rendezvous with four other Beaufighters from No. 177 Squadron. However, Agartala was fogged in when we were due to take off early in the morning, and as a result the four Beaufighters from No. 177 Squadron carried on without us. However, Group decided that we should carry out our part of the exercise just before dark. On the way to He-Ho, which is in the Southern Shan Hills in eastern Burma, the CO led us at low level over the large town of Meiktila in Central Burma, heading in the direction of He-Ho. I said to Paddy, 'I don't think that was very wise. They'll be expecting us at He-Ho'. Sure enough, as we approached the aerodrome we could see a number of Japanese fighters circling the aerodrome at low level, obviously waiting for us. The CO called up to say that we would make only one run over the 'drome in line abreast firing at anything in sight and at the same time increasing our speed to maximum, and then head west for base. By some miracle, none of our aircraft was hit by the heavy anti-aircraft fire or by the Japanese fighters, and, once again thanks to the superior speed of the Beaufighters at ground level, we were able to beat a hasty retreat without having caused much damage to the enemy.

On the way back to Agartala and with night closing in, we picked up a signal from base to the effect that the weather was deteriorating – a fact of which we were already aware, as we could see vivid lightning ahead over the Chin Hills. The CO was diverting us south to avoid the storm, but it was not long before we were in cloud and quickly lost visual contact with each other. Flight Sergeant Peacock's navigator, Flight Sergeant

Higson, went on the air to say he was not sure where they were and that their fuel was running low. He was picked up by Chittagong and directed there for a safe landing. My navigator, Paddy, said that if we could hold the course we were on, we could expect to make Comilla, sixty miles south of Agartala. When I let down after crossing the Chin Hills and broke cloud, there ahead was the welcoming beam of Comilla aerodrome, which we decided to land at as our petrol was getting very low. On landing we found Nicolson had landed just ahead of us and whilst we were being debriefed, word came through that Flying Officer Thompson had landed at Agartala. As was customary at debriefings, the intelligence officer offered cigarettes to the crews who had just landed and for the first – and only – time I accepted the offer. We had been up since 4 am for the original operation, had just completed four and a half hours of tough flying, it was after 9 pm and we were very tired.

Two days later, on 7 February 1944, word came through that the squadron was to move forthwith to Parashuram, some ninety miles south of Agartala, between Comilla and Fenni. To achieve this with a minimum of disruption to our operational activities, the Dakotas of No. 194 (Transport) Squadron – who were to take our place at Agartala, and so rejoin their 'parental' squadron, No. 31 – provided most efficient transportation for the ground staff and the squadron equipment. So well organised was the move that it was completed in two days. No. 194 Squadron had been formed in October 1942, at Lahore with Lockheed Hudsons and, with the help of No. 31 Squadron, were introduced to supply dropping and, later, conversion to Dakotas. There was apparently much celebration when the two squadrons were reunited at Agartala.

It was a sorry occasion for us all to leave Agartala after a twelve-month stay, and it was particularly sad for me as I decided it would be better to leave my monkey, Modu, with No. 194 Squadron in the environment she had come to know and like.

Early in the morning of the second day of the move, four Beaufighters, including the author's, left Agartala for Chittagong to standby for short-range low-level attacks in support of the British 15th Corps, who were having a hard time with the Japanese 28th Army on the Mayu Peninsular. The Japanese had launched their Arakan 'March on Delhi' offensive just a few days before the British were to launch their planned Arakan offensive down the Mayu Peninsular to capture Akyab. The Japanese strategy was based on a seven-day timetable, for which their men each carried seven days' rations. In the first seven days of their offensive, they planned to capture the important shipping port of Chittagong. The Mayu Peninsular engagement – codenamed HA-GO by the Japanese – was to be one of great significance to the Allies, for the eventual outcome was, in fact, the first victory for their ground forces since the Burma Campaign had begun two years earlier. Moving swiftly, the Japanese surrounded the British units, resulting in the Administrative Block Battle which lasted seventeen days and where the British Army units dug in, fought and beat the Japanese, being totally supplied with food and equipment from the air.

The role of the air forces was vital to the eventual Allied success. We made a number of low-level sorties into a very small target area along the Kaladan River, being briefed to attack any buildings or basha huts we could locate as, presumably, they were being occupied by the Japanese. Our role with the Beaufighters was supplemented by Wellingtons, carrying 4,000 pounds of bombs, and dive-bombing Vultee Vengeances, whilst overhead Spitfires annihilated Japanese fighters who were trying to reach the Allied transport aircraft. During the campaign, the Spitfires destroyed or damaged sixty-four Japanese fighters for the loss of four Spitfires. The air supply to the ground forces was carried out by Nos 31 and 194 Squadrons, based at Agartala, as well as 25 Commando aircraft diverted from 'Hump' duties and led by the American airman, Brigadier-General William D. Old. During the month of February, the Dakotas and the C-46 Commandos, often closely supported by Hurricane fighters, dropped or landed some 10,000 tons of supplies to the British ground forces; sometimes the dropping zone measured a mere 200 by sixty yards.

Whilst this activity was going on in the Arakan, the squadron quickly settled into Parashuram, which lacked the 'refinements' of Agartala. First, it only had a grass runway, which would be a problem when there was heavy rain, so we made a guess between ourselves that there would soon be another move – certainly before the next monsoon. A good feature of the runway was that it was flat and wide (200 feet), somewhat different from Agartala's roller-coaster runway. Secondly, there were no night flying facilities, so when there was a night operation we made a ten-minute hop to Fenni in daylight where we were looked after by No. 177 (Beaufighter) Squadron until it was time to take off. Thirdly, the accommodation quarters were poor – there were solid bamboo charpois for the airmen to sleep on, but the officers had to sleep on the insect-ridden floor on our own campbed kit until such time as we could build ourselves bamboo charpois. There was no local labour such as bearers, because the nearby village had cases of smallpox and to make matters worse the place swarmed with flies. We had to domesticate ourselves quickly, including doing our own laundry, fetching and boiling our own water, and so on.

One long operation of nearly five hours took Paddy and me east of Lashio where the railway from Rangoon ends and the Burma Road climbs the high mountains into China. We had Captain Pete Sanders, the Army Liaison Officer, with us as an observer, as the Army apparently wanted him to have a first hand look at what was going on in that part of the world. We had been briefed to follow the railway from Nam Yao back through Lashio and down to Gokteik before returning to Parashuram. We strafed a moving train south of Lashio and then ran into particularly heavy ack-ack fire at Hsipaw, but were not hit. Simultaneously, two other Beaufighters piloted by Flight Sergeants Peacock and Gibson followed the railway from Gokteik down to Mandalay and had also strafed a moving train and a staff car before being attacked by three Army 0.1 fighters at Maymyo. The Japanese fighters chased the two Beaufighters for twenty minutes, making occasional long-range cannon attacks, but once more the speed of the Beaufighters at ground level proved too much for the Japanese fighters.

Early in the month, Flying Officer Cotter was given special leave to represent Bengal in the All India Olympic Type Games at Patiala, opened by General Auchinleck. John, who pre-war had twice been second in the English Decathlon Championship and had represented England in the long jump, finished fourth in the discus and fifth in the shot putt – as he put it, 'well below my pre-war standard'.

At the end of February, postings came through for pilots Pilot Officer Jock Gunn, Warrant Officer Ron Thorogood and Flight Sergeant Brian Hartness. They were all posted to Poona, near Bombay, as flying instructors. A party went on all night until they caught the early morning train en route for Poona, by which time they were slightly the worse for wear.

March 1944 began with a continuation of February's hectic activity. Of the thirty-nine operations which we carried out, involving sixty-eight aircraft, fifteen were to Arakan targets and fifteen were to North Burma targets, and were directly related to the heavy fighting that was taking place in the two theatres of war.

No sooner had the British got on top of the Japanese in the Arakan than major interest swung to Northern Burma. The incredible landing of 10,000 British troops, their equipment and some 1300 pack animals under Major General Wingate flown in from Lalaghat, Assam, in eighty gliders towed by Dakotas and more than 600 sorties by Dakotas landing on improvised strips called 'Piccadilly', 'Broadway', 'Chowringhee' located 150 miles behind enemy lines, straddling the Mandalay/Myitkyina railway, began on 5 March. It was the greatest airborne invasion of the war until the invasion of Europe three months later.

The operation was supported by RAF and USAAF fighters and bombers, and on the ground by RAF aircrew officers, 'resting' from air operations, who accompanied every Chindit column, acting as spotter contact between the column and Allied fighters which were seeking out Japanese ground forces. A variety of Allied aircraft were used during the operation for supply dropping and casualty evacuation, including de Havilland Tiger Moths and Fox Moths, Stinson Sentinels, helicopters and two Short Sunderland flying boats, christened *Gert* and *Daisy*, which were landed on Lake Indawgyi in enemy territory. One injured Army evacuee, after being brought out by a DC-3 Dakota, was heard to say, 'As far as I'm concerned, sir, they can keep their VC's and MC's. Give me the DC's.'

At this time the Japanese launched their major offensive against India – which they had codenamed U-GO. They had used the HA-GO Arakan campaign as a diversionary exercise, expecting the British to commit large numbers of troops in anticipation that the Japanese would make a major thrust from the south into Bengal. Their 15th Army in the north had been built up to 100,000 crack soldiers, and with this force they planned to destroy the British 4 Corps, occupy Dimapur, a strategic rail centre on the

94

Bengal-Assam railway, and seize the 'Hump' airfields in Assam. The Japanese came close to achieving their objective, but once again Allied airpower proved invaluable during the fighting associated with the sieges of Imphal and Kohima. Early in March, on Admiral Mountbatten's orders, the entire 5th Indian Division, then fighting in the Arakan, was moved by some 750 flights of transport aircraft from Dohazari in the Arakan to Imphal in the Chin Hills and was back in action within a matter of days, this time in support of the British 4th Corps. For the first time in the history of war, a complete Division with all its equipment was flown from one battle to the centre of another.

A combination of these two totally separate army/air operations in March 1944 was a staggering effort – one that Allied countries around the world heard very little of at the time as war publicity was generally tuned to what was happening in the European, Mediterranean and Pacific theatres.

At Parashuram, we were centred between the two fronts without really knowing what was going on. Operations were concentrated in the Arakan and Northern Burma where, during March 1944, over forty motor transports, some with soldiers, and many bullock carts, were attacked on the roads. On the railways, twenty-one locomotives, at least 150 rail trucks/coaches and three bridges were attacked. River targets were mainly small craft comprising over 200 sampans and country craft. In addition three small factories, eight oil and water storage tanks and several hundred forty-four gallon drums of oil were destroyed or damaged. The weather in March had been deteriorating, giving signs of an early monsoon. Of the thirty-nine operations carried out, of which nine were by Mosquitos, six had to be aborted.

11 March 1944 was a red letter day for the squadron for, with the score at 197 destroyed or damaged locomotives, Pilot Officer Trudgeon with his navigator, Flying Officer Dobson, brought up the two-hundredth. In fact, they made it 202, with attacks on one locomotive in a shelter at Talkon, two at Kyaukse and two at Myinthi. We were all saddened when the same crew were shot down and killed by heavy Bofors fire near Taungup just four days later.

The previous day another Beaufighter and the crew of Warrant Officer Fairclough and Flight Sergeant Shaw were lost in unusual circumstances. It was their first operation and it was being led by Pilot Officer Spratt; their targets were the river and roads around Pakokku and Pauk. In rather hazy conditions, the two aircraft became separated near Chauk where Fairclough's aeroplane was last seen flying in a north-westerly direction; it is not known what became of it. Before this, Spratt, whilst attacking rivercraft, had been troubled by his number two following too closely and opening fire too soon, forcing him to take evasive action, in spite of which, his aircraft was hit five times.

During March 1944, one operation of four Beaufighters led by Pilot Officer Clegg, an Australian, was mounted to strafe a Japanese camp at Lemyethna, west of Henzada, in

Southern Burma. Accompanying Clegg as an observer was Mr Paul Chadburn, a reporter of the *Parade* magazine, whose three-page story, entitled 'Death Whispers over Burma', with photographs of the briefing, the attacks and the post-operational activities, does full justice to the operation, as would be expected of a wartime journalist.

Long range fighters, attacking communications, report one steamer sunk and a locomotive destroyed'. That was the notice the *Calcutta Statesman* gave to our op. Not even the name of the long range fighter. But the Japs have a name for it all right: they call it 'whispering death'. Behind the brief notices in the communiqués – they appear every day and are worded much alike – lies hidden a small epic, raced through at more than 200 miles an hour. I can't reproduce it properly, not being of the breed of these airmen. But here is an outsider's account.

We arrived at the squadron – a very famous one with a VC as Commanding Officer and more than 200 locos to its credit in Burma – at three in the afternoon; at 3.30 we were briefed for next day's op. Nine of us, the crews of four fighters and myself. The CO was away, but his stand-in [author: Squadron Leader Horn, 'A' Flight Commander] stripped to the waist before a large map, pointed out our target, a military camp. 'You'll find it easily by this kink in the river. You'll fly this way, over the sea, then up and across the hills here and down on to the target. After the first run it's up to Flying Officer C. [author: Clegg] (the leader) how many more attacks you make; depends on the opposition.' Several of the men were new to this job, very young they looked, unburned yet by Burma's suns. They listened eagerly, asked questions.

After the briefing, the squadron leader spoke to half a dozen sergeant pilots and navigators, newly posted, who had arrived that day. We stayed on and listened. Some points were: 'It's hell's own climate here just before and during the monsoons – 24 hours of body drip. You'll all probably get prickly heat, sounds a pretty piddling sort of thing I know, but I can tell you its not so bloody funny. By September you'll most likely be pretty near the bend; some of us have stayed round it for some time now.' (*note:* 'round the bend' equals Western Desert dottiness). . . 'When the monsoon's gathering – you understand, before the rains come, the weather's an etc. Don't try and fly through it. When you see the muck ahead, you may be able to fly under it. But don't get the idea you've come to hell's ugly spot. I'm telling you the worst, so you'll find it bloody pleasant in comparison. Bags of leave. You'll probably say now that Calcutta's a pretty lousy spot, but I've had some bloody good times there myself . . . For your first three ops I don't want sensational results. Any questions?' There was a number. Some most technical.

We spent the evening in the mess, a large basha with long chairs, a well-stocked bookcase, a proper bar with a shining row of silver tankards, presented by officers who had been posted, a darts board and a famous Line Book in which anyone heard shooting a line was duly reported: specimen at random – 'Of course, some of us don't have to shoot a line: we just tell the truth.' On the cover the squadron's arms and motto: QUAM CELERRIME AD ASTRA (freely, very freely translated, 'In which we swerve').

We drank rum and lemon, talking to an Australian officer who had strafed in the Western Desert in the early days. His opinion was the same as that of all those who had been on both these fronts: '. . . and the desert was *clean*.'

Rumination under the mosquito net, while the jackals and pi-dogs howled hellishly: 500 miles away scores of Japs were carousing or fondling their concubines quite oblivious of what was coming to them next day at a certain pin-pointed place, at a certain arranged hour . . . out of the tree-tops, suddenly, whispering death. Nine ordinary Britishers went to sleep after an ordinary evening. It seemed odd that you should be so solidly based 200 miles behind the front one day – and the next . . . the next? We didn't like to think of it overmuch.

Next morning we jeeped to the landing strip, a converted paddy field. There were our four fighters, serviced the day before. I was given a mae west, parachute, collapsible canvas canoe, jungle knife, American K rations, fishing line; a complete emergency outfit.

I climbed into the belly of the 'plane, sat down behind the pilot on the step over the trap. Ours was the leading 'plane. The pilot, an Australian on his twenty-seventh op, was a good man to sit behind on his job: quiet, efficient, cheerful. We plugged in on the intercom: 'Hello! Can you hear me? OK. Right. Contact starboard.' We circled the strip until the three other 'planes were off the ground. Then set course due south.

From a not altogether healthy curiosity we questioned our pilot about various matters creeping towards us with the hands on the clock. We learnt: that it shouldn't be a particular 'sticky' job. On the other hand, we didn't know how strongly the Jap camp was defended. If it was stiff with guns, on a second run-in the last fighter, which would be the eighth 'plane over. . .

We learnt that heavy ack-ack is pretty well useless against low-flying fighters skimming over the tree tops at 200 knots (about 250 mph). It is difficult for even the light ack-ack to swivel quickly enough to draw a bead on you. There remain trip wires, tied across railway lines, rivers, and, perhaps the greatest menace of all, Jap riflemen scattered about all over the country, in villages, ditches, reeds, everywhere. The danger is the special ring sights on their rifles adjusted to the speed of our ground-strafing fighters. They have only to get the 'plane on the edge of the ring and pull the trigger. We learnt, also, that Zeros can be a nuisance, but at low levels 'whispering death' can keep ahead of them, even draw away (orders are normally not to engage Zeros, though there have been some notable exceptions).

Now that we were finally committed it gave us a sense of relief: there was nothing we could do about it. As we flew low over the sea, the Arakan plain on the port side, a feeling of exultation came over us. Let them all come – we have good pilots, good navigators, good 'planes. We were flying on a following wind and passed by heavily defended Akyab well ahead of scheduled time. I fell into a doze, not because of indifference – probably rather the reverse. A change of course brought me to the alert. The navigator's voice came through the earphones: 'A black speck, low to starboard, seems to be coming out of *** Island – might be a Zero.' Our pilot was bringing the fighters into formation. Nothing more was observed of the possible Zero.

Soon we were making height, flying east over the Mayu foothills. Then we sailed down over the valley of Burma, and here it was that the fun began. First there was the excitement – to me – of finding the target. I stood up and looked over the pilot's shoulder at his map. But where was our river with the kink in it? There were now so many rivers, all snaking lazily across the flat land, drowsing in the afternoon haze. A bit of a poem sailed absurdly into my head: 'A sleepy land of streams.' Most inappropriately, but such things happen, and for the rest of the op. lines of the 'Garden of Proserpine', with rhyme, certainly, but with no kind of reason in the circumstances, kept recurring like hiccups. We had struck a railway line with a road that led beside it; rushing just above the ground with a dream-like feeling of invincibility, of irresistible force, as it were the prow of a ship cleaving whispering death. The peasants in the paddy fields, hearing us only when we were right on them, scattered helplessly, flopped to the ground, dived into rushes or into their bamboo bashas; men leapt off bullock carts – a target, these, when over a certain number: Japs use them to convoy supplies: others plunged off sampans into rivers ('Here where the world is quiet: here where all trouble seems dead winds and spent waves riot in doubtful dreams of dreams').

But neither bullock wagons nor river sampans were our target for today. We held on along the railway – with never a train on it, and small wonder! Clumps of trees usually meant small villages.

Flying over them we 'skidded' (slipping sideways while keeping the same course) out of respect for those Jap ring sights, although it seemed flat impossible to me, at the time, that anything at all could stop us – a dangerous gremlin feeling that probably attacks some pilots. As everyone in our way fled in terror before us, I felt both the exultation of power and simultaneously twinges of pity for the 'bods' cowering down (because I'd done it myself I suppose). In spite of the sensation of being this avenging fury, I could not understand how we could possibly find the target. There were so many clumps of trees; any one of them might hide it.

Then, suddenly, there it was, right in front of us, rows of hutments. We charged straight at them, opening up with twin rows of cannon at about 500 yards. The pilot was pressing both 'tits', cannon and camera. For a few seconds the HE shells lit up the hutments like a row of shops on pre-war Piccadilly, but smoking shops. The cockpit was a haze of sour-smelling cordite. Just as we thought we were going to crash right through the barracks, we soared up steeply.

No opposition. At least, no ack-ack. Bullet holes through the fuselage there might be. But nothing could stop us. Nothing. Circling, we saw the other fighters coming in on to the target after us. Then we went in again – again and again. Five times. There was not a Jap to be seen. A mile away, the gold dome of a pagoda shone out over the tree-tops ('I watch the green field growing for reaping folk and sowing, for harvest time and mowing, a sleepy world of streams'). Thin columns of smoke were rising out of the jungle – air raid signals.

I changed seats with the navigator. It meant that my view of things – except of possible Zeros on our tail – was limited. So that when the urgent crackle of the cannon came again I didn't see the target (it was a large storehouse that might have contained petrol). But the next target I did see. We came to a point where the railway line stopped abruptly. A large cantilever bridge was dangling in a tangled metal ruin, the work either of our sappers in the evacuation of Burma, or more recently of American bombers. Drawn up beside the river bank was an ancient-looking locomotive, nearer in design to *Puffing Billy* than *The Flying Scotsman*. Behind it a line of carriages, astir with anxious 'bods'. But our target was the loco. We shot it up four times, left it a steaming ruin. The 209th.

We had been stooging and strafing for about three-quarters of an hour. The job was well done and it was time to go back. The navigator got back into his glass blister and I with difficulty, plumped out with my life-saving paraphernalia, lurched back to my step behind the pilot.

We landed on the flare path in near darkness and went straight in to inter-ops, telling what we had done and seen to the intelligence officer, drinking pint after pint of tea. Thence to the mess and life on the humdrum level once more. To a comfortable bed in a basha where there was no danger, no exultation.

But two days later, our pilot would be off again – our pilot and the others. Another job, the twenty-eighth.

Whilst the squadron was undertaking these operational duties, a number of events took place that resulted in the squadron being taken out of operations by the end of March. There were a number of postings during the month, beginning with Captain Pete Sanders on 6 March, much to everyone's disappointment. His cheerfulness and ready wit where always a tonic in the Mess. On 9 March it was announced that all of 'A' Flight's Mosquitos and some of the aircrews were to be posted. There was an immediate replacement with Beaufighters and new aircrew and so No. 27 Squadron reverted to the role of a strictly Beaufighter squadron.

Air Marshal Sir John Baldwin, commander of the Third Tactical Air Force, paid a visit on 15 March. After giving the aircrew a review of the operations now going on in Northern Burma, presented Squadron Leader Horn, 'A' Flight Commander, with an immediate award of the Distinguished Service Order. This was combined with his posting to the Special Low Attack Instruction School (SLAIS) at Ranchi as Chief Flying Instructor. With Horn's departure from No. 27 Squadron, one of the Mosquito pilots, Flight Lieutenant Snell, took over as the 'A' Flight Commander and, rather sadly, Rupert, the remaining Himalayan bear who had been with us under 'Bunny' Horn's care for fifteen months, was sent back to Agartala where No. 194 Squadron were only too happy to adopt him. No doubt my monkey, Modu, would also have been pleased to see him as they had become very friendly when we were all at Agartala.

On 19 March, it was my turn to be posted, together with three other 'originals', Flight Lieutenant Laing and Thompson, and Flying Officer Sterling, as well as Flight Sergeant Chippendale. Before we left Parashuram, word came through that the squadron was to be withdrawn from operations and was to be relocated at Cholavaram, near Madras, for operational rest and reformation. Laing, Thompson and Chippendale were posted to No. 21 Ferry Control, Mauripore, Karachi, whilst Paddy and I were posted to No. 22 Ferry Control, Allahabad, Central India. We all agreed that we would have preferred to have gone to Cholavaram with the squadron than to begin ferrying Beaufighters, etc., around India and Ceylon, which was hardly the same as being at Cholavaram on operational rest. After our departure, the original thirty-six aircrew were down to eight, three pilots and five navigators: Flight Lieutenant Franklin, DFC, Flying Officers Cotter, House, Dinwoodie, DFC, and Flying Officer Spratt, and Flight Sergeants Johnson, DFM, Cooper and Adcroft.

During the final preparations for the move to Cholavaram, Flight Sergeant Skeen lost his life while air-testing his aircraft in readiness for the next day's flight. He crashed shortly after taking off at Parashuram, the aircraft catching fire and setting alight a number of huts in an Indian village, killing one woman.

The squadron had been on constant operational flying for a period of fifteen months, during which time it had operated from four aerodromes – Amarda Road, Kanchrapara, Agartala and Parashuram. During that period it had two commanding officers – Wing Commander H.C. Daish and Wing Commander J. B. Nicolson, VC. In all, thirty-two aircrew were killed as a result of operations, another three survived as prisoners of war and three were killed in non-operational flying accidents. Awards made to aircrew were one Distinguished Service Order, three Distinguished Flying Crosses and one Distinguished Flying Medal. The squadron undertook a total of 397 operations, of which 337 were in daylight and sixty at night. To carry out these operations, 801 individual sorties were flown – 756 by Beaufighters and forty-five by Mosquitos. Purely to indicate the number of sorties flown by individual crews, Paddy and I made thirty-six sorties.

According to official records the squadron caused much destruction and damage to the Japanese lines of communication on rail, road and river, to aircraft and aerodromes, ground installations, stores and equipment, and had a significant effect on the morale of the Japanese troops. At the time, it was difficult for the aircrews – and even more difficult for the groundcrews who were not so personally involved with the Japanese – to appreciate just what the combined efforts of the squadron were doing to disrupt the overall Japanese war effort in Burma. Without the groundcrew's tremendous and unstinting efforts, the squadron would simply not have performed so successfully. To them, wherever they are, I know that I echo the sentiments of all of the aircrew who flew on No. 27 Squadron in the Burma Campaign when I say, 'Thanks fellows for your tremendous efforts.'

9 · THE MOUNTBATTEN ERA

The appointment of Rear-Admiral Lord Louis Mountbatten (later Admiral of the Fleet, the Earl Mountbatten of Burma), formerly Chief of Combined Operations, as Supreme Allied Commander in South East Asia, was decided in August 1943 at the Quebec Conference by Prime Minister Churchill and President Roosevelt, and it came into effect on 16 November 1943. General Stilwell became Deputy Supreme Allied Commander whilst General Auchinleck retained his position as Commander-in-Chief India.

The India/Burma/China theatre was to be called South East Asia Command (SEAC), and Mountbatten was quickly referred to as the 'Supremo'. King George VI gave his consent to SEAC adopting as their device a phoenix – a fabulous and fierce bird which rose from the ashes of fire. The 'wings of the phoenix' were the newly formed Air Command South East Asia (ACSEA) under Air Chief Marshal Sir Richard Peirse, KCB, DSO, AFC. Integration of the RAF and the USAAF quickly followed, and Eastern Air Command, under Major General George Stratemeyer, was formed and divided into Third Tactical Air Force (TAF), Strategic Air Force, Troop Carrier Command and Photographic Reconnaissance Force. The combined strength at the time was forty-eight RAF and seventeen USAAF squadrons which had been built up from virtually nothing over a period of eighteen months.

Nos 27 and 177 (Beaufighter) Squadrons operated under the Third TAF, which was commanded by Air Marshal Sir John Baldwin. Eventually, there were six Beaufighter squadrons. Simultaneously with the Supremo's appointment, the first two Spitfire Mk V squadrons, Nos 607 and 615, began operating from Chittagong and had immediate success against the Japanese Mitsubishi Ki-46 *Dinahs* that had been able to operate as reconnaissance aircraft above the maximum ceiling of the Hurricanes. All in all, the Allies in the Burma theatre ended 1943 on a high note of expectation and confidence.

The Allies' initial strategy under Mountbatten was to make sure that the Chinese remained active against the Japanese in Yunnan Province, and he was instructed to secure the Burma-China Road and safeguard the 'Hump' air route to China, which was

101

to be built up to carry 20,000 tons of supplies each month. He quickly visited Chiang Kai-shek and then, with General Stilwell, drafted plans for the Churchill/Roosevelt/Chiang Kai-shek conference at Cairo, providing for a pre-1944 monsoon operation by Wingate into Northern Burma and for an amphibious landing in Southern Burma. These plans were accepted by the three leaders. However, the decision to supply naval craft for the amphibious landing was reversed at the next leaders' conference, in Teheran, when the naval craft were re-allocated to the Mediteranean to appease the Russians and were, in fact, used for the Anzio landings.

Chiang Kai-shek was not amused by the change of plans, and felt that he was now released from his Yunnan commitment. Mountbatten went ahead with the pre-1944 monsoon Wingate operation, and, at the same time, found himself deeply involved with the Japanese offensives in the Arakan and the Chin Hills, which were referred to in the previous chapter. Perhaps the outcome may have proved to be a fortunate break for Mountbatten, as the added responsibility of conducting an amphibious landing in Southern Burma could have presented tremendous logistic problems.

The series of successes against the Japanese in the Arakan in March 1944 and at Imphal and Kohima in the Chin Hills in June 1944 was the turning point of the war in Burma – for the Japanese, it meant double defeat, and for the Allies the scent of victory. The two Japanese thrusts had been reversed and their air force had been practically wiped out, and it only remained for the Allies to re-group for a major land thrust into Burma from the north after the 1944 monsoon and victory in Burma would be inevitable.

Realising that the Japanese in the Chin Hills were in a serious position after Imphal and Kohima, and that their overstretched lines of communication gave them no option but to retreat to the plains of Burma, Mountbatten decided to use the 14th Army under General Slim to harry them relentlessly and to mount intensive air interdiction operations to impede their withdrawal by destroying every bridge that they would have to use in the retreat. This policy was adopted throughout the 1944 monsoon, when 175 inches of rain fell in Northern Burma and 500 inches in nearby Assam, conditions which made both movement on the ground and aerial operations very difficult. Airfields lost a few months earlier to the Japanese were recovered, and the Hurribombers were able again to operate close to the front, supported by Vengeances, Thunderbolts and Spitfires. On the ground, the 14th Army, as they advanced back into Burma, found increasing numbers of Japanese dead.

No. 27 Squadron was still 'on rest' at Cholavaram, Madras, but the Beaufighters of No. 177 Squadron were continuing the policy of long-range low-level attacks on all forms of Japanese communication in Central/Southern Burma. They concentrated on pre-dawn sorties along railway systems to catch supply trains that had not reached the specially constructed underground daylight shelters, and on rivercraft along the Chindwin River which the Japanese land forces, retreating out of the Chin Hills, had to cross to continue their escape back into Central Burma. Once Kalewa on the Chindwin River was retaken by the 14th Army, the Allies were in a position to move out into the plains of Northern/Central Burma and were, in the words of Rudyard Kipling 'on the road to Mandalay'.

Depriving Mountbatten of his naval craft for an amphibious landing in Southern Burma – which was planned to be supported by an airborne invasion of Rangoon, involving 1,550 transports and gliders flying 500 miles – meant that an attempt to re-occupy Burma from the north had to be completely reconsidered. Fortunately, this brought the value of Wingate's 1943 and 1944 expeditions into focus. As early as March 1944 Mountbatten wrote, 'After seeing the performance of Stilwell's forces and hearing of the wonderful show which Wingate and Cochran's No. 1 Air Commandos have put up, I am becoming convinced that Allied forces could march all over Burma provided they have adequate air supply and air support.' Planning was therefore developed along these lines for a land offensive from the north to begin in December 1944, supported by certain airborne operations in advance of the main land forces – the target being the occupation of Mandalay by the commencement of the 1945 monsoon in May. These plans were accelerated in February 1945 when Air Command said that it could supply the 14th Army with all of its food and material needs for an overland advance to Rangoon. This meant sustaining 300,000 men on the ground from the air, and involved seventeen squadrons of transport aircraft. The speed-up plans went ahead without problems, Mandalay being re-occupied on 21 March and Rangoon on 2 May.

Meanwhile, in the Arakan – and contrary to expectations – the bloodless re-occupation of Akyab took place. The Japanese simply withdrew down the Arakan coast as the Allies were planning an amphibious landing on Akyab which was to be supported by dropping 1200 tons of bombs. By 22 February, the mainland coastal towns of Myebon and Kangaw and the strategic island of Ramree were re-occupied; only twenty of the 1,000 Japanese stationed on the island surrendered. The way was now open for 15th Corps with air and naval support to prepare for an amphibious assault on Rangoon, in support of the 14th Army who were advancing down Central Burma.

As a part of the offensive campaign of December 1944/May 1945, the air forces of ACSEA underwent changes, making them more static. Air Chief Marshal Sir Trafford Leigh Mallory, KCB, DSO, was to replace Air Chief Marshal Sir Richard Peirse as Allied Air Commander in Chief, but was killed while flying out to take up the appointment. His replacement was Air Chief Marshal Sir Keith Park, KCB, KBE, MC, DFC, a New Zealander of Battle of Britain and Battle of Malta fame. Immediately below him remained Major General George E. Stratemeyer, USAAF, in charge of Eastern Air Command, under which the air operations in Burma were now divided into three areas directly responsible to Eastern Air Command. In the Arakan, No. 224 Group, RAF, was commanded by Air Commodore the Earl of Brandon, DSO. In the Imphal/Chindwin/North West Burma area, No. 221 Group, RAF, was under Air Vice

Marshal Stanley Vincent, CB, DFC, AFC. In the North Eastern Zone, the US 10th Air Force was under the command of Brigadier General John F. Egan, USAAF, tasked primarily with protecting the air route from Assam to China, while, at the same time, aiding the American, British and Chinese troops in the area.

The rapid advancement of the 14th Army in Central/Southern Burma made Air Vice Marshal Vincent the air force man most responsible for the support that the air force had undertaken to give the army in its advance. Between December 1944 and April 1945, some 318,000 tons of material and 120,000 men were lifted by air.

Experienced bomber captains from the European theatre described the task of the Dakota and the Commando squadrons as the finest operational job of the war. Sir Keith Park said that, whereas in North Africa the 8th Army had advanced under the wings of the Air Force, in Burma the 14th Army advanced on the wings of the air force. And what the Supremo said was, 'The Fighter Command won the Battle of Britain, the Bomber Command won the Battles of Europe and the Air Transport Command the Battles of South East Asia.'

After No. 27 Squadron had been taken off operations at the end of March 1944 and had moved to its new base, Cholavaram, it came under No. 225 Group and, in April, was joined by No. 47 Squadron, which had flown out from the Middle East. No. 47 Squadron was a torpedo-carrying Beaufighter unit and the two squadrons were to combine as an anti-shipping strike force to operate in the Bay of Bengal with No. 27 to attack the flak batteries on enemy ships and No. 47 to drop torpedos. They combined with ships of the Royal Navy to carry out training exercises. On one occasion, Flight Lieutenant 'Snowy' Swift, DFC, with other officers from Combined War Operations in Ceylon, visited the two squadrons. Subsequently, the two Beaufighter squadrons were joined by Fleet Air Arm Fairey Barracuda torpedo-bombers. The exercises were initially on splash targets, and then against HMS *Nizam* by groups of six Beaufighters. On one occasion, an aircraft of No. 27 Squadron was forced to ditch in the sea because of engine failure; however, the crew, of Flying Officer Spratt and Flight Sergeant Adcroft, were able to escape uninjured, although the aircraft sank immediately. It was customary for the crews of the two squadrons and for navy personnel to have a conference each Saturday morning to discuss the previous week's exercises, and then to adjourn to the Conemara Hotel – all very different from the Agartala and Parashuram days.

Another of the original crews, Pilot Officer Johnson, DFM, and Flying Officer Dinwoodie, DFC, was posted to No. 21 Ferry Control Unit at Karachi, where they joined Flight Lieutenants Laing and Thompson. The squadron now had a number of new crews who had not flown on operations, so a comprehensive training programme was introduced which covered formation, night and single-engine flying, air-to-air and air-to-ground firing, Hurricane fighter and Consolidated B-24 Liberator bomber affiliation and dinghy drill exercises. In the course of my ferry duties I had the opportunity to spend a very pleasant evening with my old squadron, and after hearing how they were 'resting' I was not quite so sure that I would prefer their activities to mine.

In June 1944, Flight Sergeant George Salter, 'B' Flight's NCO Engineer was awarded the British Empire Medal. No-one on the squadron had worked harder than Salter to keep the squadron's aircraft operational, and his award was a very popular announcement. Flight Lieutenant Franklin, DFC, the squadron Navigation Officer, returned to the United Kingdom for a special navigation course. Finally, the Commanding Officer, Wing Commander Nicolson, VC, was posted back to the Third TAF, Calcutta, in charge of aircrew training. In August, he was awarded the Distinguished Flying Cross for the role he had played as Commanding Officer of No. 27 Squadron. His successor was Wing Commander J. H. McMichael.

The training and naval co-operation exercises continued throughout the very rainy monsoon conditions of 1944 until September, when the squadron moved to the Special Low Attack Instruction School – SLAIS – at Ranchi, where the aircraft were fitted with eight 3-inch rockets on racks under the wing in place of the six wing machine guns. Simultaneously, the squadron carried out a course of rocket firing. At the same time, No. 47 Squadron was transferred from Cholavaram to Yelahanka in Southern India to convert to Mosquitos. Conversion was completed in early November, and the squadron moved to the SLAIS at Ranchi for rocket fitting and training. On arrival at Ranchi, they learnt that all Mosquitos in India were grounded due to a structural defect and, after a period of inactivity, they went back to the trusty Beaufighters, rocket-equipped.

Flight Lieutenant Bill Hughes joined No. 47 Squadron at Yelahanka, having flown a Mosquito from England. He had the job of converting the Beaufighter pilots to Mosquitos, which, as it turned out with No. 27 Squadron, was a wasted exercise as both squadrons finished the campaign on Beaufighters. Bill and I joined the RAAF on the same day in Sydney, Australia, and had consecutive service numbers. We never knew that we had both served in the Burma campaign on Beaufighters and Mosquitos until we met some time after the war. Whereas my operations were tied to the 1943 and 1944 Allied offensives, Bill's were very much a part of the final Allied campaign of 1945. Bill became a Flight Commander with No. 47 Squadron and subsequently attained the rank of Squadron Leader, with the DFC.

After Ranchi, there followed a succession of three moves for No. 27 Squadron, from 21 October to 19 November. The first move was back to Agartala. By now, there were only two of the original aircrews with the squadron, Flight Lieutenant Cotter, and Pilot Officer Cooper, and Flying Officer Spratt, and Flight Sergeant Adcroft. It was from Agartala that Flight Lieutenant Talbot, No. 27's adjutant since November, 1942, was posted to No. 332 Maintenance Unit, Cawnpore.

No operations were made during the squadron's ten-day stay at Agartala. However, the aircrew were temporarily seconded to help the Dakotas of Nos 31 and 194

Squadrons on their supply dropping missions and as Wing Commander McMichael recorded, 'A bag of onions being lifted when the aircraft suddenly drops among the hills can be a very heavy weight.'

Early in November 1944, the squadron moved to Dohazari in the Arakan. John Cotter's navigator, Cooper, was posted away and was immediately replaced by another of the original No. 27 Squadron aircrew, Flight Lieutenant Bill House. On 19 November, the squadron made its third move of the month to nearby Chiringa, joining two other Beaufighter squadrons, Nos 177 and 211, operating under No. 901 Wing, No. 224 Group. So, after eight months 'on rest', the squadron was again back on operations.

One of the first operations, flown by Pilot Officer Trigwell and his navigator, Pilot Officer Chippendale, leading Flight Sergeant McDowall and Sergeant Cooper, ended in most unusual circumstances. They had been briefed to attack road transport on the Taungup Pass, between Taungup and Prome. Without warning, they were attacked over the target area by two USAAF Lockheed P-38 Lightnings. Neither Beaufighter survived the attack, although Trigwell, after hitting a mangrove tree, was able to crash land his aircraft in about four feet of water. Triggy was not injured, but Chips was badly wounded in the back by cannon shells and was unable to move. With much difficulty, Triggy was able to get Chips out. He recovered what he could of the medical supplies, including a few tubes of morphine and, by cutting up a parachute he was able to bandage the eight perforations in his navigator's back. That night, he bought a boat, but either he was betrayed by the Burmese or the Japanese had been able to locate the crashed aircraft, for they were taken prisoner just after dark. Chips died four days later whilst they were being transferred from the mangrove swamps to Taungup, and Triggy finally arrived in Rangoon as a prisoner of war on Christmas Eve 1944.

After capture, Trigwell was marched over the Taungup Pass to Prome, handcuffed and tied in such a way that the Japanese guard could pull a rope and cause much pain to his arms and back. He picked up a tick in his private parts which caused him considerable discomfort and had a bayonet dug into his back when he tried to avoid a big snake that was crossing the path. From Prome he was taken by train to Rangoon. At each station where the train stopped, he was paraded in front of the locals who were told he was one of the British who shot up engines, trains and railway stations. In Triggy's own words, 'It was terrific to see the damage on the railways.'

He went through considerable interrogation at Rangoon and was expecting the worst when another interrogator who spoke 'perfect American' said, 'It's my duty to do another interrogation – just tell me what you told the others – I hate having to do this but it is orders.' Triggy said 'You've lived in a lot of places besides Japan,' to which the interrogator replied, 'Yeah, I lived most of my life in New York, but was asked to come home just before the war started and of course I must be patriotic, but I wouldn't have come back if I'd known what was in store for me.' As he left he said, 'You will be going to a prison camp now, and I'm afraid they are not as good as you people provide for our men, but it's all they have got. I feel sorry but I have no say in them.' He was taken to Rangoon prison that day, but was later moved to a prison compound where conditions were much better.

Triggy became associated with prisoners of war from other services, such as Harold Green, a British commando, Bill Davis, USAAF, whose two years' service somehow became four and a half as he recounted his service life, and a very unpleasant Dutchman who continually complained that he never received as much rice as the other prisoners. In the course of stripping their ceiling and roof timbers for firewood, Triggy found an old table knife which was useful for making mess tins out of a zinc-coated metal sheet that served as a partition in the toilets. With extra honing to the knife, Triggy was able to carry out rather primitive and painful haircuts and shaves on any of the prisoners prepared to put up with the discomfort.

Triggy's camp had 1300 prisoners, 600 of whom were British, American and Dutch, and the rest Chinese and Indian. On 25 April, five months after becoming a prisoner of war, he was one of 400 whom the Japanese selected to be dressed in Japanese clothing and then marched north from Rangoon. On the fifth day when they were north of Pegu, the senior Allied prisoner of war, Brigadier Hobbs, informed the group that the Japanese commandant had left a letter with him saying that they were being freed and that 'they would meet us on the battlefield later'.

The 400 prisoners were now on their own and had the job of making contact with the advancing 14th Army, their main problem being that they were dressed in Japanese clothing. Over the previous five days they had been subject to considerable harassment by way of bombings and cannon strafing by RAF Mosquitos but suffered no casualties. Eventually, when they reached suitable terrain, they made from their clothing a large Union Jack and a message: '400 BRITISH POWS HERE PLEASE DROP RADIO'. In due course, they decided that RAF aircraft had spotted the signs but, much to their surprise, they suddenly found themselves being attacked by three Hurricanes with bombs and machine-guns with one unfortunate killing, that of Brigadier Hobbs. Suddenly, they found themselves surrounded by Sikh soldiers. They were quickly transported to an advance Army base and then flown back to Comilla base hospital, just sixty miles from Agartala where Triggy had first joined No. 27 Squadron. It was not long before he was flown home to Western Australia, being one of the first two West Australians to be repatriated from a Japanese prisoner of war camp. Wally Trigwell was one of five brothers who served in the Royal Australian Air Force and the Australian infantry forces, three of whom became prisoners of war and one of whom lost his life.

There are two aspects of Triggy's air force service worth recounting. Triggy himself is on record as saying, 'Let's get the record straight – I guess I would have been the worse pilot to ever fly for "27" and finished the war with five aircraft destroyed, all His Majesty's, and I still tell my friends that the RAF finally got the message and asked the

Yanks to shoot me down!!??' The other is in a letter Wing Commander Nicolson wrote to me in January 1945, when he said, 'Trig's show was indeed a tragedy, and I had some very hot words with the General himself, and won in the end. He was avenged the other night when we pulled down one of their big jobs by mistake!' So much for the fortunes of war.

Throughout November and December 1944 and January 1945, No 27 Squadron maintained its role of low-level attacks against the Japanese lines of communication with the more damaging battery of eight 3-inch rockets taking over from the six .303 machine guns. These rockets were the equivalent of a broadside from a 6-inch gun cruiser. The Japanese had virtually given up the railways as a means of transport because rolling stock was down to a minimum – in the period from January 1943 to March 1944 No. 27 Squadron had destroyed or damaged more than 200 locomotives. The main targets were now rivercraft, road transport and installations. Operations against these resulted in the loss of seven Beaufighters. One of the crews lost was an 'old', but not original, crew – Flying Officers 'Chalky' White and 'Deadloss' Cross. They were a popular pair, Chalky with his undying cheerfulness and Sam with his quiet wit. Sam was married and left behind a baby he had never seen. They were lost on 29 November. Two days later, Chalky's brother walked into the mess enquiring about him – awkward silence and awkward condolences. This was a similar situation to that one year earlier when Ken Herbert's brother had walked into the mess at Agartala shortly after Ken had been shot down.

In January 1945, Flight Lieutenant Cotter and Pilot Officer Brinded were posted to Visual Control Post Duties with the 14th Army in Burma – John protested, but to no avail. Eventually, when in Burma, he came across an ex-No. 27 Squadron pilot, Flying Officer Taylor, who had joined the squadron at Cholavaram. On three successive take-offs at Cholavaram, Taylor had swung. On the third occasion, he ripped off the undercarriage, narrowly missing nearby parked aircraft. That ended his flying career. When John came across him in Burma he was wearing the Military Cross which he had been awarded for leading the army unit to which he was attached to safety through Japanese lines after it had lost its senior officers and was nearing the end of its ammunition. The 'square peg' had found a 'square hole'.

February and March 1945 saw more changes set in train for the squadron. Primarily, the aircraft were due for complete overhauls and, to allow the ground crews at Chiringa to get on with the job uninterrupted, all of the aircrew and forty ground crew went back to Ranchi for rocket refresher practice. On 21 March, the CO, Wing Commander McMichael, was repatriated to the United Kingdom, tour-expired. On 27 March, just one year to the day since it had first been taken out of operations and sent to Cholavaram, No. 27 Squadron again ceased offensive operations after a period of four months. This second spell of operations had resulted in the loss of five aircraft on operations and six through accidents. This high accident rate was mainly attributed to the serious lack of spare parts; in fact, aircraft were only kept serviceable by 'cannibalising' parts from other aircraft.

The new role for No. 27 Squadron from April 1945 was to be Air Jungle Search and Rescue Duties, a far cry from the original role in 1943 of low-level offensive missions against Japanese lines of communication. The Beaufighters, still using Chiringa as their base, were modified to drop emergency containers from torpedo slings under the fuselage and through the exit hatch behind the pilot. The squadron was split into three sections with one remaining at Chiringa and the others on detachment at Akyab and Monywa/Meiktila in Central Burma. To assist with inter-communications, the squadron was allocated a Stinson L-5 Sentinel.

The new Commanding Officer was Wing Commander T.P.A. Bradley, DSO, DFC, but within two weeks of his joining the squadron he and his navigator, Pilot Officer Holmes, were killed when their aircraft hit a vulture, more commonly called a shite hawk, when coming in to land. The vultures were a real menace around aerodromes where they congregated for food scraps – I hit one with the leading edge of my wing over Agartala in 1943 which meant a new wing had to be fitted. The replacement Commanding Officer was Lieutenant Colonel E.T. Strever, DFC, of the South African Air Force.

As always, the 1945 monsoon rains began in May, when the squadron's base was again moved, this time to Akyab. No. 27 Squadron's role was to be on constant standby for urgent requests from the Army or RAF. Many painstaking, tedious search and rescue operations were made over the sea, whilst over the land numerous supply-dropping sorties were made to Allied forces operating deep in Japanese-held territories, such as to V Force, E Force and Force 136. No. 27 Squadron operated in these roles until VJ Day, 15 August 1945.

The Allies final assault for the recapture of Rangoon, code-named Operation Dracula, was to include a parachute invasion from aircraft based at Akyab. D-Day was set for 2 May. In separate operations, two old pilots of No. 27 Squadron, Wing Commander Nicolson and Squadron Leader Thompson, took part in Dracula which, tragically, for Nicolson was to end his life. On the same day and quite nearby, my ex-navigator, Paddy Sterling, was badly injured in an aircraft crash.

Squadron Leader Thompson, now a flight commander with No. 177 (Beaufighter) Squadron was briefed to lead eight Beaufighters on a rocket attack on Japanese gun positions around Rangoon. The weather on 2 May was extremely bad over the Bay of Bengal, and only four of the eight Beaufighters reached the target area to find, like other assault units that day, that the Japanese had already gone.

Wing Commander Nicolson was in charge of flying training at HQ Third TAF and took every opportunity to visit the squadrons for which he was responsible and to fly with the crews whose training state was his task to organise. He was visiting Salbani, Bengal, on 1 May when he attended a briefing for a Liberator attack the next morning,

D-Day, on Japanese gun positions in Burma and persuaded the reluctant squadron commander of No. 355 Squadron to allow him to fly in one of the bombers so that he could see at first hand the type of operation being carried out. The Liberator took off on 2 May at 0051 hours and at 0330 hours it radioed its position as approximately 130 miles south east of Calcutta. It was assumed from this message that the aircraft would be returning to base about 0630 hours. When it became overdue an Air-Sea Rescue search was instituted and at 1505 hours two members of the crew were found clinging to the wreckage of the Liberator. One body was also recovered but no trace of Wing Commander Nicolson or the other occupants was ever found. According to one of the survivors, one of the Liberator's engines caught fire. The bombs had been jettisoned and the aircraft had tried to return to base, but had been unable to maintain height.

Flight Lieutenant Sterling was still at No. 22 Ferry Control, Allahabad, and on 2 May was navigating a Beaufighter to Dum Dum aerodrome, Calcutta. The aircraft had developed engine trouble and was making a single-engine landing at Dum Dum when an aircraft on the ground taxied out to take off. The pilot of the Beaufighter, 'Jonah' Jones, attempted to go around again but crashed at the end of the runway – he was killed, but Paddy survived with severe back injuries which ended his flying career.

Apart from these three coincidental occurrences on D-Day, 2 May, Wing Commander Nicolson's No. 27 Squadron navigator, Flight Lieutenant Franklin, who was then No. 224 Group Navigation Officer, was drowned about the same time whilst swimming at Akyab not far from where Wing Commander Nicolson also met his death. The same Bay of Bengal – under completely different circumstances – had claimed the lives of the aircrew which Wing Commander Winfield, DFC, AFC, described in *The Sky Belongs To Them* as the most formidable aircrew he ever flew with.

With the Japanese beaten, the feeling within the squadron was that it would soon be disbanded and this duly happened in September. However, the disbanding order was almost immediately countermanded because of civil strife in nearby Java. So, instead of disbanding, the squadron found itself being moved from Akyab to Mingaladon airfield, Rangoon. After settling in at Mingaladon, a detachment was sent to Java and another to Penang in Northern Malaya. The remaining aircraft at Mingaladon continued supply-dropping sorties to the Army who were involved in mopping up operations in the Shan States and in north east Burma to the China/Siam border.

With the move to Mingaladon, uncertainty had arisen over when the members of the squadron would return to their home countries. However, Christmas 1945 was one of special joy for forty of the airmen who had been with the squadron for more than three years, for they sailed for the United Kingdom on 27 December. More postings followed, until the squadron was officially disbanded on 1 February 1946.

Wing Commander Nicolson had joined No. 27 Squadron in August 1943 as the only fighter pilot of World War Two to receive the Victoria Cross. The reader will recall the several references to the magnificent work of No. 31 (Transport) Squadron which shared Agartala with us. One of their pilots, Flight Lieutenant D.S.A. Lord, after a tour of operations over Burma which earned him the Distinguished Flying Cross was posted back to the European theatre. On 19 September 1944, as a member of No. 271 (Transport) Squadron, he was engaged in supply-dropping to troops at Arnhem. Early in his run in to the dropping zone, his aircraft was hit by anti-aircraft gunfire and began to burn. Regardless, he pressed on and dropped his supplies. He continued to fly the stricken aircraft to enable several members of his crew to parachute out, but he himself was unable to escape and was killed. He was posthumously awarded the Victoria Cross for bravery. Thus Agartala, which today is a commercial aerodrome in India, has the distinction of having had on the aerodrome in 1943 at the same time the only pilots of World War Two to receive the Victoria Cross in their respective commands, Fighter and Transport.

10 · TRIBUTE TO PADDY

I cannot think of a better way to complete the story about No. 27 Squadron than on an 'Irish note'. When pilots and navigators came together at No. 2(C) OTU, Catfoss, they teamed up as aircrews and were posted accordingly to operational duties. Paddy, as navigator, from Northern Ireland, and I, as pilot, from Australia, teamed up in July 1942. I had arrived at Catfoss six weeks earlier and had already gone solo on the Beaufighter before Paddy arrived. The navigator allocated to me on the previous course had not reached the required standard and was posted, and I found myself without a navigator. Pending commencement of the next course, I did staff flying on Blenheims and had the opportunity to gain an insight into the navigators arriving for the next course. Paddy was my choice, and when he said 'yes' to teaming up with me, a very strong wartime association began which continued until July 1944 when I was posted home to Australia. He was the baby of the No. 27 Squadron aircrew – he was nineteen and I was twenty-four years of age when we came together, and, coincidentally, our birthdays were on the same day, 18 January.

Only once in the course of the thirty-six operational sorties that we flew on No. 27 Squadron were we separated, and only then because Paddy was sick. As time progressed, he made it very clear that he only wanted to fly on operations with me – maybe that's Irish superstition – but I have to confess that it worked in reverse as I couldn't see any reason to fly with anyone else on operations – and maybe that's Australian superstition.

We lost track of each other shortly after I returned to Australia and in the course of writing the book I never succeeded in finding him by enquiry or correspondence through various channels. Therefore, it was more than a surprise when, on arriving at the Ministry of Defence, Air Historical Branch, London, by appointment on 19 August 1983, the Historian, Mr H.H. Wynn, said, 'I think we should try this telephone number in Bangor, Northern Ireland.' It was Paddy, and without hesitation, he said, 'I'll come over to London on Monday and stay a couple of days.' This he did, with log books, diary, photographs, stories and old-time humour.

He joined me for my pre-arranged appointment with the RAF Museum at Hendon, where I was handing over some memorabilia to the Museum in relation to Wing Commander Nicolson's Victoria Cross. As a result, the Museum, in conjunction with *RAF News*, photographed Paddy and me in front of the Museum's Beaufighter holding Nick's Victoria Cross. It was certainly nostalgic.

My own log book was lost – I suspect stolen – with some of my luggage during disembarkation at Melbourne in 1944, and, I imagine, finished up in Port Philip Bay. Fortunately, Paddy's log book recorded all of our flying history together, which the RAF Museum kindly copied for me. It contained the following endorsement on Paddy's departure from No. 27 Squadron in March 1944:

ASSESSMENT OF ABILITY AS A NAV/W:– ABOVE THE AVERAGE AT LOW LEVEL.
REMARKS:– A VERY SOUND YOUNG NAVIGATOR. HAS BEEN STRONGLY RECOMMENDED FOR A PILOTS COURSE. HE AND HIS PILOT HAVE BEEN ONE OF THE MOST SUCCESSFUL CREWS ON THIS UNIT. THOROUGHLY KEEN AND A FIRST CLASS OPERATIONAL TYPE.
(signed)
James B. Nicolson,
Wing Commander.

But here's the Irish flavour. When Paddy joined the RAF, he elected to become a navigator rather than a pilot because of what had happened to his father in the Royal Flying Corps in the 1914-18 war. His father first became a pilot, earning the Distinguished Flying Cross, but was subsequently re-classified as an observer, serving many years postwar as an RAF advisor to the rulers in some Middle East countries.

Paddy's reasoning when he chose to be a navigator rather than a pilot in the 1939-45 war was, 'I may as well nominate at the beginning to be a navigator rather than, like my father, start out as a pilot and finish up as a navigator anyway'! If that's not Irish, what is?

And on that note, I shall finish the story by saying, 'God bless you, Paddy'.

APPENDIX 1
IN MEMORIAM

KILLED ON OPERATIONS, FEBRUARY 1943-MARCH 1944

17 February 1943	Flying Officer J. Townsend and Pilot Officer Wandless
21 February 1943	Squadron Leader Illingworth, DFC, and Sergeant Osguthorpe
26 March 1943	Squadron Leader Statham, AFC, and Pilot Officer Briffett
4 April 1943	Sergeant Ensor and Sergeant Clough
29 May 1943	Flying Officer Sturrock and Sergeant Heywood
29 June 1943	Flight Sergeant Petch and Sergeant Thomas
15 September 1943	— Flying Officer A.R.B. Ball (navigator)
16 October 1943	Sergeant Humphries and Sergeant Bainton
14 November 1943	Flying Officer Hassell and Flight Sergeant Thomas
21 November 1943	Sergeant Plummer and Sergeant Collingwood
16 December 1943	Flight Sergeant Vincent and Sergeant Mathewson
11 January 1944	Flight Sergeant Britter and Flight Sergeant Paine
12 January 1944	Pilot Officer Gunn and Sergeant Luff
14 March 1944	Warrant Officer Fairclough and Flight Sergeant Shaw
15 March 1944	Pilot Officer Trudgeon and Flying Officer Dobson

TAKEN PRISONER OF WAR AND DIED IN CAPTIVITY

18 November 1943	Flight Lieutenant R. Williams and Flying Officer K. Herbert
16 November 1944	— Pilot Officer M. Chippendale (navigator)*

TAKEN PRISONER OF WAR AND RELEASED IN 1945

7 March 1943	Flight Lieutenant J. McMichael and Sergeant Dodd
16 November 1944	Pilot Officer E.M.W. Trigwell (pilot)* —

* Both joined No. 27 Squadron at Agartala in 1943 and became prisoners of war just after the squadron began its second tour of operations from Dohazari. See pages 106-108.

KILLED AS A RESULT OF NON-OPERATIONAL FLYING ACCIDENT

17 May 1943   Sergeant Norman and Sergeant Perris

27 March 1944   Flight Sergeant Skeen (Pilot)   —

APPENDIX 2
DECORATIONS AND AWARDS

October 1943
Distinguished Flying Cross

Flying Officer Alexander Moir Dinwoodie, RAF Volunteer Reserve, No. 27 Squadron.

Distinguished Flying Medal

Sergeant Cyril George Johnson, RAF Volunteer Reserve, No. 27 Squadron.

As navigator and pilot respectively, this officer and airman have completed many successful sorties and have displayed a high degree of skill, courage and tenacity. On one occasion they attacked and destroyed a very large oil storage tank. In addition, 12 sampans were destroyed. In spite of extremely bad weather, the aircraft was flown safely to base. Flying Officer Dinwoodie and Sergeant Johnson rendered valuable service.

January 1944
Distinguished Flying Cross

Flight Lieutenant Robert Alan Swift, RAAF, No. 27 Squadron.

Flight Lieutenant Swift has flown a large number of operational sorties. While serving in the Middle East he has taken part in low level attacks on road and enemy airfields, attacked enemy troop carrying aircraft and escorted two Malta convoys. In operations in Burma this officer has destroyed and damaged oil tanks, enemy transport and airfields. He can always be relied upon to complete his allotted tasks, whatever the difficulties to be surmounted and has consistently set a fine example of devotion to duty.

January 1944
Distinguished Flying Cross

Acting Flight Lieutenant Wallace Montague Franklin, RAF Volunteer Reserve, No. 27 Squadron.

117

This officer has taken part in many operational sorties of a varying nature in Europe, the Middle East and Burma. While in Burma as squadron navigation officer, he has successfully guided large formations of aircraft accurately to the target, through very adverse monsoon weather. On several occasions his aircraft has been damaged by anti-aircraft fire which on one occasion put the compasses out of order but with outstanding skill he led the formation back to base. Flight Lieutenant Franklin's devotion to duty, efficiency and resolution have contributed in no small measure to the many successes attained by this squadron.

March 1944
Distinguished Service Order

Acting Squadron Leader Ernest Bernard Horn, RAF Volunteer Reserve, No. 27 Squadron.

This officer has completed a very large number of sorties. He has effectively attacked two railway buildings, some 22 locomotives and many more trucks. On other occasions he has damaged or destroyed 13 small steamers, 285 sampans and numerous larger rivercraft. In operations against industrial installations, Squadron Leader Horn has attacked very many factories, a power plant and two wireless buildings with good results. This officer is a magnificent leader, whose achievements are a splendid tribute to his great skill, iron determination and unfailing devotion to duty.

June 1944
British Empire Medal

Sergeant George Salter, RAF

No citation for this award exists.

August 1944
Distinguished Flying Cross

Acting Wing Commander James Brindley Nicolson, VC, RAFO, No. 27 Squadron

Wing Commander Nicolson has consistently shown himself to be a courageous and enterprising leader. In spite of two spells of sickness caused by the burns sustained in the action which gained him the Victoria Cross, he has always been eager to fly and lead his squadron personally on the most hazardous sorties. His fine example has been extremely valuable to the squadron.

Other Awards

Three other members of the 'original' No. 27 Squadron, Squadron Leader P.A.S. Thompson (pilot), Squadron Leader J. Cotter (pilot) and Flight Lieutenant W. House (navigator), subsequently received the Distinguished Flying Cross, while Group Captain H.C. Daish (pilot) was awarded the Order of the British Empire.

Burma Star

The Burma Star was instituted in recognition of operational service in the Burma Campaign between 11 December 1941 and 2 September 1945. There were other qualifying periods for service in the provinces of Bengal and Assam and in China and Malaya.

All members of the Forces engaged in the Burma Campaign endured the discomfort of sub-tropical climatic conditions and primitive habitation. Fighting tropical diseases was as much a problem as fighting the enemy. In these difficult circumstances, a great many lifelong comradeships were established, epitomised forty years later in the 14,000 Burma Star Association in the United Kingdom, which gives practical form to the comradeship which grew and developed during the Burma Campaign.

APPENDIX 3
NO.27 SQUADRON POSTWAR ACTIVITIES

1 February 1946   Disbanded at Mingaladon; it has not subsequently returned to the fighter role.

24 November 1947   Reformed at RAF Oakington with Douglas Dakotas as a transport unit in No. 46 Group, Transport Command, RAF.

1948-49   Involved in Operation VITTLES (the Berlin airlift) and other operations.

10 November 1950   Disbanded at Netheravon.

15 June 1953   Reformed at RAF Scampton, Lincolnshire, with English-Electric Canberra B.2s as a bomber unit in No. 1 (Bomber) Group.

June 1954   Operation MED TRIP, six squadron aircraft making a goodwill tour of Europe and the Mediterranean, visiting France, Italy, Greece, Turkey, Yugoslavia and Portugal.

7 January 1955   Squadron presented with a Standard.

May 1955   Moved to RAF Waddington, Lincolnshire.

October-December 1955   Deployed to Nicosia, Cyprus, and operated against Eygptian targets during the Suez Crisis.

3 December 1957   Disbanded at RAF Waddington.

1 April 1961   Reformed at RAF Scampton with Avro Vulcan B.2s as part of Bomber Command's nuclear V-Force.

1 May 1962   Squadron mounted its first Quick Reaction Alert (Nuclear) (four-minute readiness, nuclear response).

August-September 1962   One squadron Vulcan and one from No. 617 Squadron took part in the Canadian International Air Show, Toronto.

1963   A squadron Vulcan became the first aircraft to launch the *Blue Steel* stand-off bomb in practice. No. 617 Squadron was the first, No. 27 the second and No. 83 the third unit operational with *Blue Steel*, all at Scampton.

June 1969   Squadron stands down from QRA (Nuclear) tasking.

29 March 1972   Disbanded at RAF Scampton.

November 1973 Reformed at RAF Scampton with Avro Vulcan B.2(MRR) aircraft as the only RAF squadron operating in the maritime radar reconnaissance role, involving close co-ordination with the Royal Navy and NATO maritime forces.

1976 Walt Disney Productions gave permission to use the cartoon character Dumbo, the elephant, as No. 27 Squadron's unofficial mascot.

22 June 1979 Squadron presented with a new Standard.

31 March 1982 Disbanded at RAF Scampton.

12 August 1983 Reformed at RAF Marham with PANAVIA Tornado GR.1 all-weather strike/attack aircraft (both conventional and nuclear roles).

INDEX

123

MAPS